3/20/16

Hey Bill,

Hope you enjoy it. I've appreciated our relationship and hope

Uncle Duke Gathers His Wits

Or

Truths and Heresies

W. K. Haydon

it continues. I took the liberty of a small dedication because I really respect what you have done and continue to do.

Warm regards, Duke

Acknowledgements

No part of this publication may be reproduced or transmitted in any form or by any means, electronic or mechanical, including photocopying or recording or any information storage or retrieval system without permission in writing from the publisher.

Several of these essays appeared in *The South Side Journal, Lafayette Marquis, Innsbrook Insight,* and *Cowboy Times.*

Cover design and illustration: Laura Thake Graphic Design

Library and Archives United States Cataloguing in Publication

Haydon, W.K., 1948 –

  Uncle Duke Gathers his Wits, or: Truths and Heresies

Issued also in electronic form
First Edition

Published by Singing Bone Press
www.singingbonepress.com

Singing Bone Press

ISBN 978-0-933439-08-5

If there is to be a dedication to this book, it can be to no other than Diana, Caleb and Beau Baylor. One by one they came into my life and provided me with a framework and a sense of purpose. They created a space that allowed me to pay attention to the stories happening right in front of me. Day in and day out. This has been an immense and profound gift.

And this almost goes without saying, but I am deeply indebted to my long time friend, Jerred Metz, who hounded me for years to do this book, and who finally irresistibly insisted. He also gave me my only brush with fame by putting ME into one of his books of fiction. Though he did kill me off pretty early, I thought.

As a writer/role model, I need go no further than Bill McClellan who has done fine, consistent and what I consider to be courageous work in St. Louis for a lot of years.

The TRUTH, it turns out, is a kind of maypole we dance around. We grab onto different versions of the truth and hold on hard. Till it breaks. Then we grab a new ribbon and start all over again.

Uncle Duke

Table of Contents

W. K. Haydon

I

...And So It Begins

Dear Layla

...in which Uncle Duke examines Love and Loss.

I saw a hand-made sign the other day on Highway Z. Hastily scrawled on the back of a manila envelope with a red Magic Marker, it was stapled to a stop sign. It had the definite look of desperation about it. It said: *"Layla, Layla. Please come home!"*

I was oddly moved. I don't know Layla, but there was something very sweet and plaintive in that little message. There was longing and regret and hope for forgiveness. That thing that he did...he won't do it anymore. Or that thing that he didn't do...he'll start doing it now. There were unspoken promises to do better, be better, reaching out into an unknowable future, trying to draw Layla back into it. In his vision of the future, he and Layla were side by side. They were drinking beer and doing the two-step on Saturday night, making furious love afterward and having a leisurely breakfast together Sunday morning.

Apparently Layla doesn't share the same vision. Not with him anyway. Maybe Layla wasn't envisioning no double-wide down on Bumfuck Creek in her life. Maybe she had a grander vision that would get her out of Warren County. She may already be on her way. She might already be long gone and not even looking back over her shoulder. She might never even see his stupid sign. It would be, in my opinion, a damn shame if she didn't.

I try and drive by every day now to see if there are any updates in the saga. Is the sign gone? Did she come back? Are there any additions, any further inducements? "I promise I'll change!" or "This time I'll do my share!" Are there any responses? "Are you through messing around?" or "Not in this lifetime, Bucko!" Or maybe a whole set of proposals and counter-proposals, a legally binding, pre-reconciliation agreement. In this Internet Age, here is a lover's manifesto stapled there to the stop sign, on the aptly named Highway Z–the Highway of Last Resort. The End of the Road. On a post usually reserved for notices of garage sales and lost dogs, someone makes a profound, sincere request. For all to see. A post normally dedicated to traffic and order has temporarily become a romantic beacon, a public forum for broken relationships. At one of life's busy little intersections, across the road from the 7-Eleven, there's a Lovers' Last Stand. It was touching somehow.

I suggest that it was a humbling gesture, putting up that sign. I am personally impressed. That area is a small community, made up mostly of trailer parks and itty-bitty track homes. There are some large suburban homes making their way in that direction. But none of those folks put up that sign. I don't see some guy with a two-car garage and a Great Room putting up a plaintive note like that. No way.

See, it's likely that a lot of people around there know Layla. Consequently, they know who put up that sign. And now they know she's left him, and that he's rattling around in that trailer all by himself, a man abandoned, hoping for her return. That's his voice stapled to that stop sign. They'll recognize his low-down cry: "Layla, Layla. Please come home!" 24 hours a day. Till the last of that red ink bleeds on down the post.

Being together is hard. Living with another person is a convoluted journey, with lots of little decisions which determine whether we make it or not. And there are many things over which we have so little control. What we mean as an act of kindness and affection can be misinterpreted. What your Daddy did might not be what your Lady wants. What you need ain't always what you get. Sometimes there's someone to blame for your sadness, and sometimes there isn't.

Money, sex, time. There's generally not enough of any of them. But sometimes there's too much of one or the other. Which can somehow be worse.

The outside world acts on us more than we act on it. Consequently, there's generally a fair amount of pressure. Then we have our pasts to carry around. At any one moment it can overpower the present. Our futures are often haunted by people and things that used to be. It is hard enough to sort out our own stuff. Somebody else's stuff in the bedroom complicates things exponentially. It is not a simple multiplier. It's not just times 2. Combining lives, sharing a bed, squares the degree of difficulty. Cubes it maybe. Even the short hauls can be hard. The way I see it, the odds are long.

But I've always rooted for the underdog. And I like happy endings. So I'm hoping she comes back. I urge her to give him a second chance every time I drive by. My sense is that there is real penitence there. I think he's learned a valuable lesson. There is considerable humility and even some optimism in his tone.

He needs you, Lady. He recognizes that now. And, Layla, to be needed is almost as good as being loved. It's close. And he may even love you. Though that's very tricky to know for sure. Love is a word we often use to get what we want. It can be a manipulative technique. Sometimes it's shorthand for lust and just complicates the discussion. I mean, I believe in love, but it's a hard word to parse. You got to examine it close.

I don't know. Love can be a wonderful thing. At its finest, it has the power to transform meaningless, joyless lives into things grand and rich and full. Even in its lesser forms, it can make a boring existence terribly interesting. It can add passion, drama, conflict...and sometimes, glorious resolution.

And that's what I'm hoping for Layla and her anonymous friend...Resolution! Something grand and rich and full! Because there's lots out there that isn't that. We hear about it, read about it and personally see it and feel it every day. Anger, resentment, frustration. And it's just sad is all. We deserve better–every one of us. Every mother's son. Every father's daughter. It grows on trees, but we can't pick it. It's thick as pollen, but we can't collect it. We can live without it. We know that. We've done it before. Often for long stretches. But we shouldn't have to. It's less than we deserve.

Eternal Rest for $39.95

...in which Uncle Duke discusses his interment.

It has come to my attention that there is a guy in Alabama who is marketing a do-it-yourself casket kit. It sells for $39.95 and can apparently be used as a bookshelf or a coffee table while you wait. He calls the approach "shop before you drop." Well I don't know about you, but my confidence in the market place just went up several notches. Hallelujah! The American entrepreneurial spirit lives. Finally, a product to fill a need instead of a product on which the hucksters have to spend $millions$ creating the need. Finally, a serious inventor not involved with athletic shoes.

This is definitely an idea whose time has come. The American way of interment has never made a whit of sense to me. It has always seemed to me that intricately carved mahogany caskets and ornamental bronze caskets are pretentious and grandiose at best and a serious waste of money and resources at worst. Would you, on your deathbed, go out and buy a vintage Cadillac with opulent appointments and chrome hubcaps? Not likely. Would you then request that you be buried in it? Of course not. Your heirs would have power of attorney so fast it would make your catheter spin.

So what's involved here? Prestige? Do you see many senior citizens wandering through casket showrooms, whispering to each other: "Ooh, how about this baby! Look at that powder-blue chiffon headrest, will you. And I like those stainless steel handrails too. They never rust, you know." And do you see casket commercials on TV golf tournaments telling us how moisture proof and mildew resistant their new models are? Hear any silken voiced announcer say: "Go ahead. Spoil yourself. Spend the Hereafter in a spacious Perpetuity Cruiser. You've earned a little elbow room." You tell me.

Does this actually have anything to do with the deceased? Absolutely not! They have their eternal rewards. And lying in a luxurious hand-tooled box wearing their best suit and no shoes is not one of them. Old Jake hadn't worn a suit since his youngest boy married, and we're stuffing him into a new pin stripe so he can meet his Maker looking like a lawyer. Well if he hasn't made His acquaintance before now, a good tailor won't help. Uncle Phineas squeaked real hard when he lived. You don't think he wouldn't really squeak if he knew you'd spent $40 of his money for a tie he's only wearing publicly for a day and a half?

No, we're not talking about honoring the dead here. We're discussing appearances and major guilt. You walk into the display room, your loved one still lukewarm, and the guy says: "Well you could choose this simulated bronze model with the polyester interior for only $2500..." But after all they did for you, he implies, why not a refrigerator carton? Good question. Why indeed. My point entirely.

These current caskets are ecological hazards. Designed to purchase some fraction of eternity, they will not rot, rust or decay. At our current rate of population growth, we will soon need practically every square inch for tanning salons and Federal prisons. To intentionally bury things that will never go away is nuts, prevailing cultural opinions notwithstanding.

But if caskets are bad, prepared corpses are worse. After we get 30 ounces of formaldehyde pumped into us, we would normally need a special permit from the EPA to get into a toxic waste dump. Legislators however make exceptions for deceased members of their own species. You can never tell when we might rise and want to vote.

It just doesn't make very much sense to me. We say "dust to dust", but we don't really mean it. We spend most of our lives eating things that just died. But when it's our turn, we want to enshroud ourselves in something impenetrable and stay out of the food chain. No fair!

I personally think of myself as fertilizer for the Ages, and I'm mostly content with that. Oh, I'd like a ceremony as much as the next guy– with plenty of lamenting and hand-wringing, singing and fevered dancing and eulogizing to beat the band. I just don't see the need to be buried like a pharaoh.

That's why I'm so thrilled to hear about a comeback for the pine box. It's a healthy trend and serves a useful interim purpose. Such a deal! My check is in the mail.

The History of S*X, Part I

...in which Uncle Duke pokes and prods the origins of sex.

When you think about it, this whole sex thing is really very odd. We're talking about a lot more than just sperm and eggs here. There are biological, social, psychological, historical, political and religious ramifications. It's a very involved subject. I don't understand how something so elementary could become so convoluted. But boy, has it ever!

In biological terms, sex is about reproduction, about going out and multiplying. And cell division is actually the most efficient way of doing that. You just split yourself in two. There is less stress on the organism. It eliminates the need for locomotion, competition, singles bars, etc., all of which are energy intensive and expensive. And let's face it, it is easier to tango alone. There are fewer variables, fewer distractions.

In the real world, some primitive life forms still depend on self-replication for perpetuation. Bacteria, the most prevalent and successful life forms on the planet, are among them. But when we reproduce ourselves, there is little change occurring. We make copies. We do not create diversity. And the Universe invariably favors diversity. So we have evolved to reproduce by combining our gene pools with someone else's. Genetic recombination. Shuffling the deck. This is the origin of sex. Nothing very complex there yet, eh?

Snails do it. Crabs do it. Octopi do it. Even trees and shrubs do it. Sometimes it is romantic and gentle, sometimes mechanical and awkward. Sometimes it is long and languorous, and sometimes brief and violent.

There are so many forms of it. Most fish simply ejaculate over the eggs that the female has laid, casting their sperm upon the waters, as it were. Where's the thrill in that? Yet the male will posture, fight and even die for the opportunity. For arachnids such as black widows and scorpions, the instinct to mate is apparently overwhelming. For the male it is often his final act–a glorious ending, I admit. And a romantic gesture. But an ending nonetheless. To die for, as they say.

It seems pretty obvious to me how sex evolved to be so pleasurable. That thing which brings about perpetuation of the species had to be made pleasurable. Those species for whom sex was like drawing blood didn't propagate long, or often, and subsequently died out. On the other hand, it is

8

likely that those of our predecessors who enjoyed it the most did it the most. Although they wouldn't have perhaps understood it at the time, this would have led them to have more offsprings who in turn would likely have enjoyed it more and therefore done it more...etc, etc. You get my drift? Although there are other selection factors involved, it is clear to me that those who were the best lovers would tend to be our progenitors. Eh, voila! We are the culmination of 1000's of generations of sexual and sensual refinement. Congratulations! You were born to LOVE!

But the right to mate, with whom, and how often...? Now the plot thickens. Now is when we start thumping our chests and driving fast cars. Now is when we start to develop ornate plumage, style our hair and work on our abs and pecs. Now it gets interesting. Or complicated. Depending, I guess, on your perspective.

This was all originally about reproduction, about procreation. Occasionally it remains so. But a very unofficial poll on my part reveals that that is not often the case. The Catholic Church tried to restrict the experience to intentional procreation. They are still trying to rebound from that one. It's one thing to ban meat on Friday. It's quite another to ban recreational sex. The Pope stepped on his scepter there.

It is without a doubt a prime mover in our civilization, and in all previous civilizations. As far as I can tell, as soon as our bellies are full and we are warm and dry, we begin thinking about it. Not overtly perhaps. Not every minute. But there are undercurrents in all we do. Women paint and powder their faces, perfume themselves and create cleavage where there was none before. Men wear gold chains and animal skins, ride big phallic motorcycles and build big, phallic buildings. None of these things are done for survival. Nor for spiritual enlightenment. These are not religious rituals. They are done to make us more attractive, more desirable. These are done for physical and sexual enhancement, pure and simple. Deny it if you will.

Sex evolved with the different organisms. Mating habits changed with the varying species. And it is curious to me that humans evolved to mate face-to-face. Our primate ancestors (and all other mammals, as far as I know) evolved using the rear entry method. At some point we turned around to face each other, belly-to-belly. This was a momentous anthropological shift, more than just 180 degrees. It seems to me much more profound and consequential than the opposable thumb or the development of tools. I suspect this subtle little rotation led directly to the development of language. It seems clear that we developed language and began to communicate in more complex ways in response to our sexual positioning. I personally believe we learned to speak so we would have something to say to each other post-sex. It is a delicate, transitional moment. We must rapidly change gears from wild and guttural to sensitive and caring. It can be awkward. This kind of intimacy required something profound, something cerebral, something well thought out. "Hubba, hubba" just wouldn't do any more. Even for comfortable partners, it is a moment in which a beautiful experience can be spoiled by an inappropriate comment. It required language, so we made one up.

This is a big, complex topic. TO BE CONTINUED...

Mr. Jolly's Clock

...in which Uncle Duke remembers his mentor.

My mother's father, Mr. W. D. Jolly, had a unique perspective. He was hardly what you'd call an optimist. His views on the human race were not, as a rule, favorable. He was, however, a 'half-full' kind of guy.

This was particularly true with regard to household appliances and the like. He came from an era in which things lasted a lifetime. Where most people would see "broken" stuff, he would see things that "needed repair". It was a subtle but very substantial difference. He saw devices that, with a little assistance, had their functioning lives mostly ahead of them. As they suffered breakdowns, he would attempt to nurse them back to life, like a sick calf. He treated them with great care and affection. "Ain't hardly nothing wrong with it," he'd say. This would generally belie the fact that the machine would not perform the task for which it was created. He wasn't talking about output here. He was talking about Totality. What he meant was that 99% of the parts in that sewing machine were fine. It was just some little spring or 59 cent doo-hickey in there that needed replacing.

Generally, there was considerable opinion within the family that he get rid of the offending appliance. This was particularly true if it had been to his workbench more than once. He was a certifiably good fixer, but in truth his repairs were not always permanent. His repair parts were seldom factory approved, and his methods were mostly trial-and-error.

Most things in his house needed to be jiggled or whacked to get them started or keep them going. The radio needed a good solid thump on the right side to come on. To get the front door to open, you had to lift up on the door knob and kind of hump it with your hip. The dryer door was held shut with a bungee cord. The lawn mower wouldn't start til you took the air cleaner off. You had to push the toaster handle down three times before the bread would stay down. No more, no less. Somebody was always yelling: "Grandpa, the toilet won't flush!" "Lift up hard, then push down," he'd yell back. And it would always work. He was like an interpreter for mute machines. He understood their language. And he didn't try to force his appliances to live by his rules. He understood and lived by theirs.

This lifestyle demanded a fair amount of patience. Mr. Jolly had a sufficiency of that. The starter went out on his truck, and it was at least a year before he got around to replacing it. He just always parked on an incline and popped the clutch. Fortunately, there were plenty of hills around, and his emergency brake worked fine. "Gravity's more dependable than a starter," he posited. "Cheaper too." He was a man who, either by inclination or necessity, never seemed to be in much of a hurry.

He often took walks around the perimeter of the town dump. This was a form of relaxation for him and a source of spare parts as well. He was astounded at things people threw away, and as often as not he'd come home with treasures.

I remember the clock he brought home. It was a standing brass figure of a cherub or something, buck naked, his little talley whacker sitting there for all to see. He had curly hair, and he was doing some kind of ballet thingie. The clock was in his belly. Mr. Jolly saw this thing glinting in the sun and was immediately drawn to it. He waded into the pile, picked it up and cleaned it off. He knew art when he saw it, and this was a find of the first order.

He then looked at it mechanically. It seemed to be intact, so he wound it lightly. It immediately began to run like...well, like a clock. He brought it home like he'd found a Tiffany lamp, polished it up a bit and gave it a place of honor on the mantle.

My grandmother, Mrs. Jolly, was less thrilled than he. "It doesn't have any hands," she pointed out. This was technically true and had not in fact entirely escaped his notice. But it dampened his enthusiasm and affection for the clock not a whit. It was a perfectly functioning clock. Never mind that it didn't actually tell time. By this point in his life, he was less interested in time as chronology anyway. It was more of a philosophical concept. He grasped more than most that time was relative. That clock satisfied his temporal needs perfectly. He loved to hear its rhythmic ticking. To the day he died, he wound that clock everyday. "Best damn clock I ever owned," he crowed.

Well it about drove my grandmother crazy. She had her own distinct views on art. And that clock was well outside the parameters. And, as it turned out, she was more of a stickler for function than my grandfather. Everything in her house should pull its own weight, she reasoned. And that clock on her mantle, ticking so smugly but refusing to divulge the time, was beyond useless. It was useless and bragged about it. It took pride in it!

She would have thrown it out, but the dump was obviously not a safe repository. Mr. Jolly would just have found it again and probably uncovered something else even more tasteless and less useful in the process. No, that clock came with the territory. I can hear her sigh even now. She did that with some regularity.

In truth, there were other parts of the territory she was not overly fond of. Whacking radios and jiggling toilets was not a way of life she would have chosen. It lacked a certain refinement she was used to. But to my knowledge, she never even mentioned it to Mr. Jolly. She determined early on that if tolerance was a virtue, her husband (and, by extension, that clock) was her ticket to sainthood. She may have made it too. Though it didn't seem to have given her much temporal pleasure. I suppose her rewards were in the Hereafter.

My grandfather on the other hand derived great pleasure from junkyard finds and household maintenance. The price appealed to him, that much was true. But it was more than that. They appealed to his sense of cosmology, I think. The Universe was a place in which nothing ever really got thrown away. And it was his job, his particular human skill, to put things back together to serve their original, intended purpose. Or, if not, then to amuse. To do both at the same time was High Art.

Mr. Jolly certainly had a talent in that regard. We have inherited a number of his artifacts, and they have the definite stamp of the Artist. They kind of work, and they are oddly amusing. My suspicion is that he would judge that a thoroughly acceptable epitaph.

Praise Your Juices

...in which Uncle Duke looks deep, deep inside.

The subject of bodily fluids has come up for me on more than one occasion this winter. In a family with a one-year-old and a six-year-old, a woman in her childbearing years, all in the middle of flu season, it's pretty hard to ignore. There are fluids of every color and consistency oozing, dribbling, squirting from someone's orifice most of the time. I must say I had never noticed how plentiful they were. Actually it has inspired in me a newfound respect for the human body as an efficient, disease-fighting machine. I never noticed before how abundantly we eliminate waste. At one point this winter, I myself was coughing, sneezing and honking up about 50% of my body weight daily in fluorescent phlegm. It wasn't pretty, but I was deeply grateful and thoroughly impressed. It was a fairly amazing performance by a body under siege.

It seems to me that human beings are by and large ashamed of our own waste products. We would prefer to pretend that we didn't have any. We'd like to think of ourselves as purely cerebral and spiritual beings. That we harbor more nasty germs, bacteria and pathogens than your average septic tank is not part of our self-image. It is evidence of our animal past. Something we'd just as soon not think about.

[Note: Humans have over 400 species of bacteria which inhabit their digestive tract alone. They number in the trillions and weigh three to four pounds. Just thought you'd like to know.]

Altogether, it strikes me that this lack of acknowledgement is an unhealthy sign and a rather overt form of self-contempt. We smear on cosmetics and man-made fragrances to mask our own scent. We glop on stuff which effectively undoes several million years of evolution by blocking our sweat glands and diminishing the body's capacity to cool itself and release toxins. This so we won't, God forbid, offend anyone.

Most of the animal kingdom uses urine as a means of identifying their territory. It is a type of signature, a proud banner. We, on the other hand, go into seclusion for days after we eat asparagus. When we go in to move our bowels, we isolate and barricade ourselves and then spray, fog, deodorize and otherwise fumigate so whoever follows us in will not realize that our bodies are working in the exact bleeping way they were designed to work.

It's never made any sense to me that we buy an incredibly expensive dinner, savor the experience, cherish each morsel, and then are totally shamed and disgusted with the end product. What goes in must come out. And if we respect the one, we've got to respect the other. It's a mathematical, biological and psychological fact. You can look it up.

We should be proud. If we can jump high or run fast, we get plenty of praise. And elimination is just another physical skill. But stink up a bathroom and see how much praise you get. People think you're sub-human and eat road kill. Au contraire! Those who do it best live happier, healthier lives. They did a study. I saw it on the Internet.

I think perhaps the time has come to be proud of our waste products. After all, those of us who are good at it have a much better chance of passing on our genes and playing a role in the 30th Century. Which is the whole point of being here, unless I'm way off. Why do you think dogs spend all that time sniffing each others' rear ends. They're looking for indications of superior digestive systems. Good teeth and a full head of hair may help you get a date, but it's efficient elimination, well-packed feces and a good white corpuscle count that will serve us better in the long run.

Actually it strikes me that we are most of us secretly fascinated with our own waste. We feign disgust because society expects it. But we clandestinely examine it to gauge our health. And it is wise to do so. It is a measure of our mortality, that is for sure. Who has not inspected their own earwax or sniffed their belly button lint? Who among us has not examined their goobers or pondered their stool? Which one of you has not smelled your own farts with some satisfaction and affection? Confess now! Do not be ashamed, America! To love your own waste is to fully love yourself!

If we had our way, really, we'd discuss them, analyze them, with total strangers. But in today's culture, it is an indelicate topic. That's one reason why health care costs are out of control. It is OK to tell your doctor every detail about the products of your intestinal flu. It's encouraged. That's their job. But it's damned expensive.

I fully believe that one reason we are compelled to marriage is to have someone with whom we can freely discuss our unusual excretions. As far as I'm concerned, this is the definition of intimacy.

I understand that as the Boomers get older, constipation and its remedies are becoming increasingly mainstreamed in advertising markets. Laxatives are a growth industry. So just as we brought sex and the body out of the Victorian closet, we'll demystify human waste and remove the stigma from elimination.

I foresee, as the population bulge moves into retirement villages and upscale rest homes, prime time specials on The Amazing Bile System, infomercials on miracle suppositories and "National Geographic Explores the Alimentary Canal." It's just around the corner. It is Our Destiny.

We will see a gray-haired Oprah interviewing a guy who brought home videos of his intestinal transplant. And a portly Bob Villa demonstrating the care and cleaning of a colostomy bag. I tell you, I have seen the future and it is not in denial. It is a population that celebrates its wastes. So stand tall, America! Praise your juices! We are indeed the sum of our parts.

Entropy Happens

...in which Uncle Duke entwines physics and sociology.

This entropy thing explains a lot. Entropy is the principle that all things tend to disorder. It turns out it is one of the immutable Laws of the Universe. It has to do with the Big Bang, the expanding Universe and some other things which happened before most of us were born. It's not really our fault, you understand, but we're not discussing fairness here. We're talking Ultimate Laws of the Universe. Largely these have nothing to do with fairness. The painful truth is that things fall apart. Murphy's Law exists. And it is in fact defined and predicted by the Laws of Thermodynamics. And your father told you it was just your attitude.

The 2nd Law of Thermodynamics states that the entropy of an isolated system always increases. The definition of an isolated system can be extended to include this galaxy, the earth, Montana, your basement or your silverware drawer. They will, over time, go from a state of higher order to lesser order. The reason for this is fairly obvious. There are many more forms of disorder than order. A jigsaw puzzle, for example, has only one arrangement of perfect order. But it has virtually an infinite number of disordered ones. Each one is just as likely as the perfectly ordered one unless we input massive amounts of human energy. The long and short of it is that chaos is the preferred state in the Universe. And as long as the Universe continues to expand, we will continue to approach Absolute Chaos. Many of you with kids knew this intuitively.

Entropy is akin to gravity. In this atmosphere, gravity pulls everything toward the center of the earth. We know this. We've known it for a long time. Yet we persist in stacking things one atop the other, higher and higher in most cases, and then are distressed when they fall down. This is a pattern of ours. Well, in the same way, it is apparently our assigned task in this life to put things together and try to keep them together while entropy inexorably pulls them apart. Now there is admittedly a certain amount of job security inherent in this. But on a daily basis, it is a hard-to-swallow lesson in futility and darned hard work to boot.

Not only that, but our efforts to order our little corner of the Universe will contribute mightily to disorder in the rest of the Universe. For example, let's say you memorize this article. God knows why, but just pretend.

The order in your brain would increase by about 1000 words or units. However, while you were doing this, you would have converted several hundred calories of ordered energy, in the form of food, to disordered energy, in the form of heat, which you would then lose into the atmosphere by convection, sweat, etc. This process would increase the disorder in the Universe by about 10,000 million, million, million units. It's a hell of a price to pay, it seems to me. Balancing your checkbook may be a satisfying and empowering thing to do, but not if it increases the disorder in the Universe by a factor of about a hundred gazillion. The cost/benefit just isn't there.

But if there's one thing in this world that we are absolutely intent on, it's Order. We'll hire consultants. We'll pay any price. From our daily schedules to our desks to our gardens to our glove compartments to our accounts payable, we are bound and determined to set them up into a system of higher order. Our 40-hour weeks are now into the 50's and 60's as we try to systematize and categorize, align, segregate, track and collate. And in this digital age, we can organize things we had no idea we wanted or needed to organize. Whatever "it" is, there's undoubtedly an app for that.

But there is something about the Universe that abhors a database. The Laws of Entropy dictate that they will eventually crash as unseen forces scatter bits from here to the Big Dipper. The same laws of entropy hold for computers, by the way, as for our brains. An ounce of order is transformed into megatons of disorder. Over time, in all things, entropy will prevail.

I might add that the 2nd Law of Thermodynamics further states that when two systems combine, the entropy of the combined systems will be greater than the sum of the individual systems. This explains certain difficulties inherent in the marital state better than I've ever heard it put. We are searching for our answers in self-help manuals when we should be browsing physics textbooks. Living with another system is hard, it says. Be ready to input lots of energy. There are equations that apply so they can quantify it if you like.

You may be looking for a point here. The point is that we seem to be living in this world as if we make up the rules. The point is that the rules already exist. They're pretty obvious for the most part, but we largely ignore them or think we can overcome them if we only work harder. So we're always running up hills and swimming against the current. We can't even die well unless our affairs are all in order. We move stuff around, but Nature redistributes it as soon as we're done. The more order we try to impose, the less we have. The point is that entropy happens. And it's not just a good idea. It's The Law.

Men With No Names

...in which Uncle Duke learns about Respect.

I've almost always idolized winos. In a way. I know I've regarded them with considerable respect and contributed to their causes regularly over the years. I imagine them as romantic poets, overwhelmed by the futility of it all. Touched intensely by the sheer beauty of the Cosmos, they became spiritual vagrants. Scourged regularly by the sheer tragedy of events therein, they became wandering, homeless souls.

It's been my impression that the World that most of us managed to negotiate daily, that we had managed to accept as imperfect but tolerable, was imperfect in the extreme and intolerable to them. In my view, they were less ascetic versions of the wandering monks, the Samanas, the Holy Men whom Siddhartha followed for a time. They were not so much seekers though as hiders. What they sought was not enlightenment but oblivion. Though at the root of it, it's all the same suffering. They were driven to blot it all out–over and over.

There was a time when I was a misplaced and misbegotten soul my own self, and the World wasn't making a lot of sense. It was more than a little imperfect. It jangled and rattled around hollowly. It seemed to reward the scalawags and punish the pure of heart. There was a war going on, as I recall, and some talk of me becoming part of it. That was disconcerting. My future was tenuous, and I was, in Simon and Garfunkel's words, "distracted and diffused".

The discordant nature of things forced me to look into those hollow, blood-shot eyes that I so often saw on the street corners. And I recognized the fear. I understood the pain that made drink seem like the only alternative. Alcohol takes us away from the burden of being ourselves. "It ain't easy being me," is what I heard them say. And I could see that that was so. They were out there feeling the pain. They seemed to be paying dues for the Unmindful, and I anted up freely. They seemed Brothers in a tortured vision, and I gave up my spare change gratefully.

I suppose as much as anything else I appreciated the honesty. They knew they were tragically flawed. They didn't perhaps understand the why or the how. But they knew the Universe had asked them some pretty tough questions that they flat couldn't answer. They failed the midterm and dropped the course. They saw it in big, bold letters every frigging day: WITHDREW FAILING!!! Consequently, they were forced to accept, even embrace the humiliation. They were sure enough bottom feeders

I conjectured that this all had to do with the brain. It seemed to me that the World continually pumped out individuals whose brains were slightly different from everyone else's. I still believe that. As a species we continue to evolve in minute ways. Just as our bodies are all different–tall, dark, sharp–short, pale, round–awkward, graceful, hairy, petite– so our brains are all physically unique. The wiring is highly individualized. The pathways are infinitely diverse. So that we all perceive the World differently. Events are interpreted from a different perspective. The World is not at all an objective place. From our perspective we believe it is because what we see has the sense and feel of Ultimate Reality to it. There is something of the Absolute about it. But all Worlds are different, seen through other's eyes and interpreted by their brains. One man's pleasure is another's pain. Reality is a vision seen differently on everyone's personal screen.

And just as there are visible physical abnormalities, there are invisible ones. Synapses that are cross-wired. Or that are perhaps open-ended. They go nowhere. For whatever reason. Nature just likes to experiment. Some go awry, and some are wildly, eccentrically successful. Like Vincent Van Gogh. Like Bobby Fisher. Like Jerry Lee Lewis. There are aberrants, mutants, whose minds are at once beautiful and hellish, brilliant and a tangled nightmare.

I always imagined winos' brains to be like that. It seemed to me that their degree of sensitivity was dialed in too high. So that the world was too jarring. They required considerable anesthesia. They found themselves in negative territory most of the time and were bound and determined to get back to zero as fast as possible. And stay there. Which is what alcohol does better and quicker and more cheaply than anything else. And I did not begrudge them that vice.

By way of example, most towns of any respectable size have a town drunk. And to our credit, we had ours. Understand though, there were plenty of drunks there. Hundreds of them, I bet. Men mostly, out in the open, but plenty of women behind closed doors. It was a dry county, but there was no shortage of alcohol for sale. They drank hard. But they generally made it to work every day. They had wives and mothers and brothers who propped them up and bailed them out and saw to it that they wound up in their own beds at night.

Bobby Goat Simpson had no such support system. He was somehow homeless in a town where everyone had their own bed. He slept I think in various tobacco warehouses, serving sometimes as unofficial night watchman in big, drafty tobacco warehouses where there was nothing to steal. As he walked from place to place in town, he displayed a long, loping gait; and he always carried a big, old duffel bag over his shoulder, full of heavy stuff. He wore a tattered, broad-brimmed hat pulled way down over his eyes and had animated conversations as he walked. Bobby Goat had plenty of company apparently, but it wasn't anybody you could see.

It was a curious relationship, him and us. You see, in small towns, everyone has a role. Bobby Goat Simpson had perhaps one of the more important ones. He was He Who Could Go No Lower. Why, he was in fact his own figure of speech, as in: "...crazier than Bobby Goat Simpson" and "You keep that up, you'll wind up like Bobby Goat." In our town, he was Absolute Zero. That was his value. He protected us from the bottom. If we fell hard, if we collapsed entirely, we knew we would still fall on top of Bobby Goat. He was the bottom of our barrel.

I only knew him to ever have one job. That was cutting the grass at the Catholic Church. It was a big lawn, with the church way up on the hill, and he was always drenched and looking pretty peaked when he got done. We'd look up from playing ball and laugh that it sure looked like ol' Bobby Goat could use a drink. No one ever called him anything but "Bobby Goat"–even us kids who said "yes, ma'am" and "no, sir" to everyone white and over 25.

No one, that is, except Fr. Blandford. He was as fine a man as there was in that town, a humble and respectful servant of all people. And he always referred to him as "Mr. Simpson". This was a quietly revolutionary act in that town. This was a brave and decisive gesture, one that only a man with the pre-eminence of a parish priest could get away with.

The first time I heard it, it took me by surprise. It was like hearing oddly combined words thrown together in a sentence. It was a mild shock which somehow changed my whole perspective. That simple reference transformed a comical drunk into someone worth considering. It opened the curtains slightly. Just enough to allow me to look into those eyes, under that deep brow. And there wasn't anything at all comical there. There was just a lot of fear. A mountain of pain.

The Human Race is a marvelously large tent, but it turns out there are those who just don't fit. There are those whose answers are perhaps brilliant, but they don't match the questions. They are somehow out of kilter and answer questions that no one asked or that we'd just as soon no one did ask. They make us nervous. They frighten us. They are, in the end, too weird for us to handle.

In our town's case though, it may have been the other way around. For someone with their eyes open, we would have been pretty weird and frightening our own selves, with our concealed vices and separate-but-equal institutions and all. And Bobby Goat had his eyes wide open. That's the way it looked to me anyway. Besides the fear and pain in those eyes, there was also a stark and fierce and persistent intelligence. Our blind spots may have been too cavernous and chilly for Bobby Goat to live up close to.

Looking back on it, I give him credit for carrying the Dark Side of our town, for perhaps seeing what we refused to see. There's always a price to pay for that kind of vision. It's a heavy burden. I suspect it was our Dark Shadow in that duffel bag. I can't know for sure, but I believe that Mr. Simpson was a Holy Man that we just couldn't recognize. Now Fr. Blandford, now he was a Holy Man even I could recognize. I am thankful, Sir, for what you helped us see.

The Ultimate Answer

...in which Uncle Duke discusses his Favorite Things.

I like breasts. I'm not sure why. But I do know that I have liked them since I was a little boy. I would hesitate to call it a lifelong obsession. But it has been what you could call an enduring fascination. As a boy I was less fascinated by the sexual act itself than by access to breasts themselves. They were titillating, true (What's the derivation of *that* word?) but they were more than that. Breasts were mystical, magical things. Beyond reach. Untouchable. Girls had them. Boys didn't. Breasts were Power. Breasts were Big Magic. Girls had It. Boys didn't. They were great equalizers in the schoolyard balance of power. When the moral training and religious upbringing was all stripped away, it was the possibility of sharing a pair of breasts that made us be polite to girls. I hesitate to say it, but it was the promise of access that induced us to civility.

As you might imagine, I have a theory about this fascination. As my generation came along, breast-feeding fell out of fashion. It was replaced by formulas derived from dairy products. Our mothers were nutritionally replaced by Holsteins. Their nutritious, distinctive mothers' milk, enriched with naturally occurring vitamins, minerals and antibodies was replaced by vapid, pasty, all-the-same formula. And there was a tactile separation as well. Their warm, supple nipples were replaced by cold, gummy rubber thingies. And the soft, pliable breast itself was replaced by hard, brittle glass and plastic. I'm sure Freud would have had a lot to say about this if he'd known about it

At any rate we were deprived children. Sure, we had electric trains and baseball bats and bicycles, but we were nevertheless deprived. There is something about starting life at your mother's breast which is warm and loving and reassuring–something which remains with us throughout our lives. Over and above the nutritional and immunological advantages, there is something about nursing which fixes us in the center of the Cosmos and tells us we are terribly significant. At the breast, we are in the parlor, there is a fire in the hearth, we are surrounded by love and attention. All is well. With a baby bottle, we are in a chilly wing of the house being raised by hirelings. We might as well be getting it out of a soda machine, buying it by the six-pack. "Hungry?" the hireling sneers. "Grab a can out of the fridge. If you want it warm, nuke it yourself." It is our birthright, as mammals, to suckle. To be deprived of it is to perpetually seek out the withheld breast in sleazy video stores and with inappropriate partners.

Size is not an issue by the way. In this country, colossal has always been synonymous with quality. I beg to differ. Not with breasts. Large is good. Small is good too. The circle is perfect, and breasts are perfectly round. They are circles within circles. You can't get any better than that. Magnitude is only good for display purposes. You pay more for your Double AA Large in the egg department, and DD cups may be worth more in the pornography trade. But day in and day out, for what-you-call your working breast, A's are just fine. Size is no advantage.

It is curious that breasts have come to have a double function in child rearing and sexual foreplay. It is my feeling that the latter is a recent development. Unless I'm mistaken, cow udders do not play a major role in bovine foreplay. Biologists do not report that any species of ape or monkey is really very much interested in the female's chest. All of their interest lies in the business end of the beast. That's where all the coloration is. Their erogenous zones seem to be very specific and are definitely below the waist. Humans as far as I know are the only species which pay any attention to breasts as anything other than mammary glands.

The evolutionary record is sketchy on this, but if breast were anywhere near as important to our prehistoric ancestors, you'd have seen a lot more of them depicted on cave walls. My theory is that they became important in the sexual realm either right before or right after we began to cover them up. Historically, that which you can't see becomes desirable. When you shield things, you simultaneously mystify them—and they become objects to crave. One might even say lust after. Also, you protect parts of the body from the elements, and they become more sensitive. One might even say stimulated. Voila! Heck of a theory, eh?

Present day humans on the other hand glorify the breast. It has become the center of sexuality. On this planet, in this culture, bosoms have become one of the Four Great Attractors, along with Power, Wealth and Fame. Men desire them and pay gazillions every month to look at magazines and videos and live shows which feature them. *'Boobs On Display'* is big business. Culturally, it is frowned upon. Politically, it is viewed as sleaze. But in the Market Place, the real world, they are big bucks. In movies, one full-frontal flash is worth huge box office bucks. Hollywood executives could probably give you an exact dollar figure. Men will risk any and all of the other Three Great Attractors for a glimpse of the Fourth. It is an amazing thing.

Women want them too. They are Power. Breasts demand Attention. The cosmetic surgery industry bounces merrily along on breast augmentations and implant procedures. Health risks be damned. We'll sue later. Self-images are boosted, shoved, hoisted, squeezed and uplifted by push-up bras. Miracles are bought and sold every day over the counter and through the catalogs. The lingerie business is booming with subtle padding and under-wire support. Structural engineers have found whole new career opportunities, working for people named Victoria and Frederick.

I haven't even touched upon breasts and the advertising industry–the Breast as tool, the Breast as icon. You want to sell cars, tacos or trash bags, a little cleavage goes a long way. It is a no-brain thing. Show Me the Hooters! Dangle some pendulous ta-ta's on the screen or on a billboard and you are in business.

The more I think about it, breasts may be THE Great Attractor, with the first three being simply things we acquire to bargain for the latter. It may have to do with the 'Earth as Mother' metaphor. I don't know. I don't try to make sense of it. It just makes me crazy. All I know is this: Breasts are The Answer! I forget the question.

Bilbo's Journey

…in which Uncle Duke roots for all those on a Quest.

So here's the story. You may know it. Bilbo Baggins and the 12 dwarves are in the Cave of the Dragon. The dwarves are there to recover the treasure that was rightfully theirs. Their inheritance from generations past. The dragon stole it all and killed most of their ancestors years before. It is a treasure of the first order–gold and silver and inlaid jewels of all types. Exquisitely crafted and artfully fashioned, they are splendid weapons and efficient tools and a pleasure just to look upon. But the Dragon sees none of this. He hoards the treasure in his dark and loathsome cave. He neither spends it nor appreciates it. It is his alone to hoard. He sleeps upon it and fouls it with his breath. That others want it is enough.

The previous night, the Dragon, in a dreadful display of anger, sealed off the small entrance the adventurers used to get in. There is now only one way out. Through the main entrance. Which passes through the Dragon's main lair. I might add that the Dragon (this may go without saying) is immense. He is ferocious and fierce and covered with impenetrable scales and, oh by the way, breathes fire. He is also terribly intelligent, cunning, unconscionably cruel and always hungry. What to do, what to do? Survive or die, Mr. Baggins?

Bilbo is a reluctant warrior. An unlikely hero. A so-called burglar who has never burgled. He was hoodwinked, shamed and scammed into this ill-conceived adventure. He and his little band are overmatched, and the odds are long. Bilbo is now thoroughly frightened and quite sure that he will not survive this quest. It is, in fact, very likely that they will all die, that they will all be buried in the belly of the beast.

It strikes me that Uncle Duke is not unlike our poor friend Bilbo. He did not volunteer for a Quest. He was drafted. He was conscripted, dragged, spirited away from his safe home with thick walls and his cellar filled with tankards of ale and flagons of wine, only to be put in harm's way and forced to enjoin a fight against a formidable Dragon of sorts. This Dragon sleeps upon Duke's self-worth, his energy and creativity. It robs him of joy and anticipation. It is only in Duke's not having them that the

Dragon finds his pleasure. And since the Warrior Duke is slack and out of shape, he is most often overmatched. Now he finds that the only way out leads up to and through the Dragon's ghastly breath and fearsome flames. And there is no guarantee that he will survive the ordeal. It would be easier if the outcome were preordained. Some assurance would be nice. But there is no script, and practically everyday our hero wakes up with the taste of fear in his mouth and does not know for sure whether he will make it through another day.

But we know Bilbo's destiny. The author has foreshadowed it, and fictional adventures seldom end with the heroes dispatched by villains and traitors. We know that Bilbo will live. With honor, in fact. He is convinced otherwise and is acting out of instinct and driven by sheer terror. But he surpasses himself. He has depths of which he himself is unaware. He has capabilities, a capacity for action, which had lain dormant all those years. In the darkest of times, he reaches for his courage and his wit. And to his surprise he finds them ready and sharp. He has a good deal of luck as well, but we give him that as counterbalance to some unfortunate circumstances into which he unluckily fell. He is a decidedly good egg, is Bilbo, and we root for him against those long odds.

As I am rooting for old Duke–the out-of-shape warrior with the bad knees and bad hips (which we now learn were worn down by all those years without self-nourishing love. They were, we now see, joints abused and cartilage starved for their own compassion.) He was acting, if not wisely, at least by the dictates of his own conscience. He was reacting to a set of rules which had been handed down to him, modeled by generations of men who marched straight ahead and bore pain like burros bore packs. Because they were good at it, they did it for a lifetime. Because it did not kill them right away, they did it til they died.

I root for him because he is a thoroughly decent son-of-a-bitch who deserves better. I root for him because he has some talent in describing where he's been and how it felt to be there. And he has shown, of late, some capacity for honesty. Which has caught even him by surprise. I judge that to be a worthwhile trait in the world at large, in this world of men who speak mostly half-truths, if any at all. I believe he would use these talents for the betterment of Fellow Travelers. He says he would; and, this day at least, I do believe him.

We hope he rediscovers his fierceness in time, in time to confront the thick skinned Dragon and demand that which was his by birth, by rights, by the power invested in Him Who made us all.

They say that those of good heart carry the day. They say that those who seek shall find. They say that the Powers of Light overcome those of Darkness, and that Love and Trust surpass Fear and Doubt. And that Warriors will prevail. Let us hope that it is so.

II

Found Stories

P-p-f-f-f-t!

…in which Uncle Duke examines the Fine Art of Farting.

There is a researcher in Colorado who has spent twenty years study-
ing cow flatulence. I find that amazing. What is even more amazing though
is that he reports that cows emits 200 to 400 quarts of methane gas a day.
That's each and every cow! In case you don't have a calculator handy, that
comes to about 50 million malodorous metric tons per year. Sheep, water
buffalo, goats, camels, llamas, deer, elk and caribou are other major of-
fenders, but cows are the worst. It turns out that cows are contributors in a
significant way to the Greenhouse Effect, the potentially catastrophic
warming of the globe. Wouldn't that be the pits? We avert atomic holo-
caust and nuclear radiation only to be done in by dense clouds of cow farts.
What irony!

I guess I am also somewhat amazed by my own fascination with
waste gases. I've always thought of them as one of Nature's funniest phe-
nomena. But others seemed less amused. That's perhaps understating it.
No, they were embarrassed, disgusted. Embarrassed if it was them, disgusted if it was me.

I've never understood that reaction. I mean, this guy in Colorado says
humans put out about a quart of gas a day themselves, so it's not like no
one ever toots. Literally everyone is walking around everyday silently
making wind and pretending that they didn't, looking around and trying to
blame it on someone else. I know how these things work. In grade school I
sat next to Beano Spalding who, besides having the gastro-intestinal system of a billy goat, was kind of a rectal ventriloquist. He would throw ab-
rupt, raucous noises in my direction and then look over at me like I was
some kind of lagoon slime. Sr. Agnes Marie would always nail me cause
I'd laugh the loudest, and I'd wind up staying after school writing "*I will
not make rude, disgusting noises in class*" several hundred thousand
times. This accounts in part for my penmanship.

Outside of class, however, in our own private boy company, farting
was high art. There were those who could biff on command, and they were
always fun to be around. I could never stay mad at Beano 'cause things
were never dull around him. There is nothing like a well-timed mega-fart

to bring a little levity to just about any occasion. We recognized that belching and farting were the grandest and funniest things in the Universe and we did so at every opportunity, never muffling what could be amplified. On summer nights, in each other's backyards, we'd rock back and light our emissions, sending little blue poofs of flame into the air. No fireworks before or since were ever so entertaining.

Even reproductions were funny. When Nature failed us, we'd spend hours practicing uncouth sounds with our hands, mouths and armpits. If musical instruments could replicate embarrassing bodily noise, we'd all be symphony musicians now. I always felt there should have been some national competition for proficiency in simulated honking, a sort of Star Search for underarm bleaters. Those who were best at it were seldom rewarded elsewhere, that's for sure.

Girls never cut any cheese. Not out loud anyway. They didn't seem to take as much pleasure in it as we did and certainly never made as great a display of it. I've never been to a pajama party, but somehow I find it unlikely that they stayed up late judging and grading each other's burps and farts in length, magnitude and aroma like we did. I never did know how they amused themselves actually, or what they thought was funny. But like I say, I've never pretended to be a particularly good student of women.

So I admit it. Loud, inappropriate noises make me laugh. And if they are accompanied by a certain degree of rankness, well so much the funnier. It's one of those things I just never outgrew. Why others frowned and were revolted I never figured out. Another example of my arrested development, I guess. I was ashamed. I stifled myself and feigned disgust. I thought I was just weird.

Until my boys came along. I noticed from the first that they found them hilarious as well. We are kindred souls, yes indeedy. Beau Baylor giggles, guffaws and heehaws when he makes bubbles in the bath. Caleb snorts, chortles and snickers when he rips one accidentally. They can't stop laughing. And neither can I. They're chipped off my block, for sure.

So I've reevaluated. I figure now that we are the only real innocents left, the only true archangels with an undiluted sense of humor. We are probably normal, and everyone else is suppressing the desire to biff and whiff and laugh till the tears come streaming down. After all, if it weren't funny, who's been buying all those whoopee cushions all these years?

Backyard Reflections

...in which Uncle Duke examines his prejudices.

I hate starlings. They are coarse, rude and unattractive. They are awkward on the ground and inefficient in the air, the most inelegant of birds. Robins on the other hand wear evening coats and have that proud, well-planned little hop that is so endearing. And pigeons, pigeon-toed though they are, walk with some deliberation, some apparent forethought. Starlings blunder about awkwardly, in haste, with no particular pride.

They have no song, no melody. Their call is largely of squeaky notes. It is monotonous and uncreative. Even blue jays, loud and abrasive as they are, are distinctive, even individual. Starlings are monosyllabic, crude. Their call is more a belch than a song.

They are a humorless bird, intent only on the task of feeding. Gulls do not tend to laugh at themselves often either. Besides that, they are rude, raucous and mostly shameless. They thrive around mountains of garbage. But gulls are capable of such lyrical flight, such grand soaring, that I am willing to forgive them their bluster and lack of social graces.

Starlings have no such saving graces. They are scavengers of the first order. Not that I have anything against scavenging. Most of my wardrobe was acquired that way. But they are entirely unselective. Now vultures, vultures are not only unadulterated scavengers but astoundingly ugly to most eyes. To top it off they are perceived as malodorous, unkempt and totally without manners. I would argue with that perception, but even if it were true, somehow I would not hold that against them. Perhaps if I had dozens of them in my backyard on a daily basis and got to know them up close and personal, I would learn to dislike them as well. But they drift aloft, and I can admire them from afar. I envy them their perspective actually. Besides that, I feel buzzards choose their profession and take a certain amount of pride in doing it well. They may be buzzards, but they are, by God, good at it. They are well trained and ideally suited for their work. I respect them for that. Starlings on the other hand are unskilled, inefficient, largely unprofessional and apparently without scruples.

Blackbirds and crows are not the rarest of birds, nor overly polite.

They eat all manners of things and tend to congregate in giant, unruly flocks as well. But blackbirds are sleek, well groomed and appear to take a great deal of pride in their appearance. Some have even added a dash of red for flair. And crows, though no slaves to fashion, have a certain dignity, an air of intelligence. Native peoples honored them for that and included them in their legends. Starlings appear bereft of style, dignity, brains and, by all appearances, ethics. They are bullies and cheats and petty thieves. All they do is reproduce. I will say they do that damned well.

In my youth, I shot them by the hundreds, perhaps thousands. I would use them for target practice with my .22. In the summers they would flock by the millions in the large maples and elms in our town. I would fire both barrels from my grandfather's ancient 12 gauge and dozens would fall to the ground. And each one I shot made the world, in my view, a better place. To this day I am unapologetic. There is nothing redeeming about them. Where are the hunters when you really need them? Out shooting sand hill cranes or snow geese, no doubt.

The worst of it is, they are aliens–or, as they say, an introduced species. They're not even from here. They were European in origin, uninvited guests who took over the continent. English sparrows have done the same. I am not terribly fond of them either, but they are at least less offensive. Less obtrusive. Starlings on the other hand offend me in all possible ways. Of other objectionable critters, mosquitoes at least give bats something to eat. Mice are cute when they're little, and rats are useful in the laboratory. Nothing eats starlings or benefits in any way from them that I can see. They just crowd out the more refined species. Why the hell are they here, and why wasn't I consulted?

The case against starlings is in fact so strong that I fear I am missing something. Although everyone has blind spots, I myself, due to years of dedicated self-absorption, have few. I can't think of a one. But, as I say, everyone has holes in their awareness. And I will admit that if numbers are the measure of success in a species, then starlings are extraordinary evolutionary successes. Their population explosion in the North America at least is really rivaled only by the Human Race. They have found an ecological niche and filled it to the brink. They are first-rate omnivores and opportunists, again rivaled only by Humans. Seldom found in wild country, they colonize wherever people settle. In essence they prefer civilization and follow Man wherever he goes. Their history in the United States is closely reflected by our own. There are, it turns out, some broad and striking similarities.

Well, there is wisdom that says that what we hate outside of ourselves is merely a reflection of what we dislike inside ourselves. I believe that. And I confess that I hold broad elements of humanity in disrespect. What I do not understand, I tend to fear and sometimes hate. It is a blind spot. It's a hole in my soul. It is a lesson I have yet to learn. And I suspect that until I learn to respect all manners of Men, I will not fully appreciate the World. It is painfully apparent that until I learn to love starlings, I will not be fully whole.

Angela Unchained

...in which Uncle Duke directs a movie.

So this lady came in to the Y yesterday, while I was doing my machine workouts. Mid-forties maybe. She was, by my account, an attractive woman. Dark features. Nice eyes. But by today's cultural and physical standards, she was way lumpy. She was, in the parlance,...*Reubenesque*. Not obese really, but probably bigger than she'd ever been. She should have been to the Y a long time ago, but no doubt there was a lot of stuff going on in her life. And she really wasn't 'fat'. She just needed to lose a few pounds. And then it was a few more. And then she got to be 'overweight', and it was a long way back. A long way to climb. And she'd forgotten how to work out. Or maybe she'd never needed to do it before. Didn't know where to go. Didn't know how to get back what she had. Or rather, she didn't know how to get rid of what she didn't used to have. It got complicated. I think her name was Angela. It seemed like maybe her name could have been Angela.

I was imagining a variety of diets. A lot of magazine articles promising results in 3 weeks. Or 10 days. *Guaranteed!!!* And some of them might have even worked. For awhile. She might have gotten close to her cheerleading form once or twice. But those diets are so hard to hold on to. We practice self-control, we eat sensibly, we buy the expensive stuff that is good for us–cereal that tastes like baling twine, pudding that tastes like drywall compound. And it just gets to be a drag, you know. It works pretty well, but it's such hard work and we deserve better than that. We deserve some pleasure in our lives, damn it! A little treat now and again. Rewards for our hard work. A little something sweet. Don't we? Sure we do.

Well, it turns out that that weight doesn't really disappear. Not really. It might go away, but it just hides out, out there in the biosphere. That's what hers did anyway. It waited for her to get a little lazy, a little complacent. I swear, she put a little half-and-half in her coffee and ate one teenytiny truffle at that party and all that weight just rushed out of the atmosphere and got sucked back into her butt. *Baaall-llooned*, she did. One stop at Ted Drewes on her sister's birthday and her breasts got as big as cantaloupes again. And all those cute little clothes she'd just bought got put in a big old cardboard box and went down to the basement. And she got so depressed that she ate a whole bag of Oreos and washed them down with a big, old Pepsi Cola. Full strength!

And that's how she came to be at the Y at 6:30am. That's the way I read it anyway. I could see it in the way she looked hard at those machines. She was pissed. She resented having to be there. Damn genes! Mostly on her mother's side. And damn babies too, all grown up and moved away now. All those meals she made and sampled, all those pancakes, all those big, fat sandwiches with gobs of mayo, the birthday cakes, all those meringue pies she now wore round her hips. These were not her bleeping pounds. Not all of them anyway. But she had to admit that they were in her pants, and she had decided it was time to go to work. "Let's get this Fatty Farm Show on the road, by God" she muttered. Or I think she did.

But it turned out she didn't really have much of a plan. She was having some difficulty with the equipment. A lot of times when people come to the gym for the first time, they talk to one of the trainers who gives them an introduction to the equipment and a program to start with. But you have to ask. And that's embarrassing. You have to admit you have no idea what you're doing. Who wants to do that? What you want is to swing onto the machines and act like this is Day 1000 of the Kick-Ass Regime. "Step away from the Pendulum, Folks. There's some serious calories gonna get burnt here! These machines'll get HOT."

But that's not what happened. What happened was she kept getting on the machines backwards. Or trying to push down instead of pull up. Or starting the exercise before she unlocked the mechanism. It was an inglorious beginning to the first day of the rest of her life. And I wanted to tell her, very discretely: "It's OK, Angela. Change is hard. It gets easier."

It is hard. It's not impossible, but damn close. And I lied about that last part. Easier??? Hah!!! Even when we're fed up and ready to transform, we've been doing it this way forever. Even if we burned our bridges and have a reasonable plan, we don't know any other way. It's so easy to fall back into our old habits. It's the dreaded default mode–the way we've always done it! If our plan doesn't work, we get discouraged and depressed, angry and resentful, and we cash it in. Back in The Ditch we go. If it does work, if we struggle and strive and catch some success–Woo-Hoo! We're cured! Healed! Sober! Clean! Straight! Thin! Lord God Almighty. Saved!

But now that we're Saved, why would we want to continue to do these awkward, uncomfortable, painful maneuvers, every day? The whole point is to get fixed so we can go back to the way we've always done it, so we can get back into our comfort zone. Am I right? Wrong, Sister! That's how we wound up in The Ditch in the first place. Remember! Girl, if you do what you've always done, you get what you've always got!

Yowzah! I was in the Zone. But I don't think she heard much of it. I kind of mumbled, and she was a little preoccupied. But what I really wanted her to know was that I was proud of her. Yes sir, I was. See, I know how hard it is to flip the switch. I know a thing or two about getting a reluctant slug out of bed. To get here is no small accomplishment. And I wanted her to succeed. I really did. I was watching her struggle, and I kept seeing Rocky Balboa strapping on his Converse All-Stars on that first cold day in Philadelphia. "Yo Angela. Listen up," I barked. No. Not really. But I did begin to hum the movie theme. Very low..."getting stro-o-ong now...gonna fl-y-y now." Barely audible, above the clank of the machines and the hum of the gym. I was hoping she could hear it.

Looking for a Model

...in which Uncle Duke shirks responsibility for certain off-spring behavior.

I have noticed of late that my son has begun to imitate me. This is disconcerting. I have not had much practice at being a role model and haven't in fact devoted much of my time to that end. He's only 5 and deserves better.

It is difficult enough steering my own ship without worrying about what kind of example I'm setting. I never had a little brother and thankfully lived far enough away from my nephews so as not to pass on, directly at any rate, many of my bad habits. Now, however, someone in my own house is paying attention and assuming that the way I do things is *"The Right Way"*. Boy, talk about your rude awakenings.

Of course it's futile to encourage sons to do what you say, not what you do. It is likewise wasted energy to point out more proper individuals for them to emulate. Young boys always make poor choices about who to act like. It's just really embarrassing that he's choosing me to be his bad example.

Actually I can't say that I wouldn't want him to be like me. It's just that little kids shouldn't try these things yet. They lack a certain refinement. Now I've devoted a lot of time to my bad habits, cultivated them over the years and learned to be discrete. Little boys in particular can master the acts easy enough. It's the discretion that takes some seasoning.

For example, it is a well-known fact that relieving oneself in the great outdoors is one of life's most satisfying moments. I have personally marked my trail over large expanses of this great land and consider it a laudable accomplishment. And as a good father, I've passed this male tradition along. Caleb realizes that it is something profound and remarked upon it just the other day. "Dad," he said, "there's nothing like peeing on a tree, is there?" It brought a tear to my eye, I'll tell you.

However, he lacks somehow a socially acceptable grasp of what constitutes the wilderness. He tends to interpret it rather loosely. I have yet to successfully define the difference between the great outdoors and urban

41

landscaping. It's just a matter of scale however, and I'm confidant that time will work it out. The Cub Scouts might help too.

Along the same lines, he has finally grasped the difference between peeing in the shower and peeing in the tub. The one, I kept telling him, was efficient time management; while the other was abandonment of long term goals in favor of short-term necessities. I get those confused myself.

It is always a lesson in humility to see your own bad habits on display. This happens with some frequency when you have kids. I see Caleb out in public using the one-finger method of nose blowing and usually try to pass him off as one of the neighborhood urchins. Not because of the practice itself, you understand. I preach that a clean handkerchief is a valuable possession and should remain sanitary if possible for use as a headband or a tourniquet maybe. No, what embarrasses me is that his fundamentals are poor. His timing is bad, and he seldom takes the wind into account. We hope to get this straightened out before Little League.

I have mentioned before that he is fond of rude, raucous self-ejected noises. And I have sincerely tried to be properly adult in this regard. But I just can't bring myself to be morally outraged and lecture on breeches of etiquette and the evils of turpitude. Would if I could. Can't.

I guess I can't say in the end that I am not a little flattered that he tends to model himself after me, that his dress and decorum follow my own somewhat, that he has shown an interest in fairly tasteless ties, poorly knotted. Truth be told, I am substantially proud. But I realize that this is a fleeting phase and that soon enough he'll be going to wild extremes to differentiate himself from me.

I'm just thankful that in this neighborhood there is such a plethora of substantive, up-standing men and young men from whom he can model. I'm also thankful that there's plenty of the other kind too—artists, beatniks, stargazers and cowboy poets. When one is modeling oneself, the more choices the better.

Foreskin Envy

...in which Uncle Duke grieves for his lost Thingie.

I was circumcised when I was a couple of days old. I'm not sure why. No one asked my permission. Had they asked, it is doubtful I would have consented. Even at that age, it is unlikely I would have allowed anyone to strap me down and, without anesthetic, slice off some very well attached and sensitive parts of my anatomy. I may have been young and naive, but I wasn't stupid. Even then. It galls me even now that they cut off a perfectly good foreskin.

And for no good reason. This circumcision business all began with the anti-masturbation hysteria of the late 1800's. Later, in the early part of this century, there were some cancer scares. These proved to be ground-less. No matter. By this time more and more babies were born in hospitals where there was apparently an overabundance of high paid help with scal-pels. Thus, circumcision became almost a mandatory operation. Which it still remains. For no good reason. I don't get it.

Thousands of generations of evolution didn't bring about a useless little doohickey on the end of the penis. No, sir. It has a protective func-tion, kind of like an eyelid. You don't see doctors slicing off eyelids be-cause they trap dust from time to time, do you? Do they rip out your fin-gernails because they can get dirt under them? Hardly. Do they dig out your toenails because there's a chance they might get infected? Negative. No one would stand for it.

But the penis is another matter. No one wants to talk about it because it might indicate that you had an undue interest in it, which of course eve-ryone does. But everyday most boy babies routinely undergo partial ampu-tation for 19th Century medical reasons and no charges are filed. I just don't get it.

See, the head of the penis was never intended to be an outside organ. It is made of tissue similar to the inside of the mouth. The foreskin is of much thicker, less sensitive skin and is designed to protect the head. It's only after the outer skin of the head becomes desensitized from constant contact with diapers and jockey shorts that it takes on the appearance and

43

texture of outside skin. Sexually, the head is more sensitive if the foreskin is intact. You'd think that in America, of all places, where optimizing the sexual experience is a valid life-goal, there'd be rioting in the streets. Nope. They say do it, and we do it. ***Question authority??? Hah!***

Fifty years ago doctors were removing tonsils as a matter of course. They'd harrumph their way thru the explanation, that is if anyone ever asked for one. When's the last time you heard of anyone having their tonsils removed? When's the last time you heard of a tonsil? I'm not sure they even exist anymore, inflamed or otherwise. Who's ever seen one? They never gave them back. When they ceased being surgically removed, billable items, they disappeared from the vocabulary and even the anatomy charts. Hmm! I smell conspiracy here!

Breast-feeding is a parallel issue actually. The most perfect and efficient form of feeding small children, it provides for both mother and child physically, socially, psychologically and spiritually. Mammals have only been nursing their young for a couple of hundred million years. And in a generation we turn it into a misdemeanor. What am I missing here?

It has all the characteristics we require in a household appliance–it's cheap, easy to clean, comes completely assembled and doesn't require batteries. Yet there is a cultural bias against nursing that is broad and deep. Breasts are more a part of this culture than hot dogs. But try to breast feed at the ballpark. You'd get less attention fornicating at home plate. It is perfectly acceptable and indeed encouraged to pad, plunge, prod, cleave, push up and in general expose a breast for vanity's sake or other valid reasons such as advertising. But use them for what they were intended and you are threatened with public indecency. I'm definitely out of the loop on this one.

But this has happened before. Society actually does this to me on a pretty regular basis–it changes the rules, bans reasonable behavior, encourages the inane. Whenever cultures get nervous, they tend to try to improve upon nature. In so doing they invariably subvert the Natural Order. It is fairly predictable. And it really shouldn't surprise me that the male and female external organs most associated with sex are surrounded by myth and misconceptions. It just frosts my nuggets is all. If they wanted to slice off their own foreskins, well they have my permission. But I wasn't done with mine. I still miss it.

Good Medicine

...in which Uncle Duke recalls laughter fondly.

My father died of Alzheimer's disease. It was a slow process and was terribly sad to watch.

At one point when he was in the hospital, he was even more disoriented than usual. He couldn't find the bathroom. He couldn't figure out how to put on his slippers.

One day during his stay there, the Wethington brothers came to visit. They were from Campbellsville. Otis ran the mill over there, and Roy had a motel, I think.

Anyway, they had been fishing partners of my father's for years. Every Spring, Daddy, the Wethingtons, Troll Young and Uncle Stump would go down to Cumberland Lake for a week. Crappie mostly. Every now and again a smallmouth.

Otis and Roy did not come to the hospital to visit a sick man. They didn't come in hushed tones with shuffling feet. They came to visit an old friend. They slapped him on the back, they insulted him and told off-color jokes. They talked about the Lake. "I don't know who was a worse cook," Roy said, "you or Stump." "I don't believe I ever had my fish scrambled quite the way you did 'em," Otis added.

They came in laughing and left laughing. And Daddy laughed with them. He had a big old grin on his face and insulted them back. For a time, while they were there, he looked like he could get dressed and go back to work.

He couldn't of course. His time had passed. But for an afternoon, the Wethingtons brought him back to life. Their laughter made his shoulders shake and allowed his brain to work. It did not last long, but while it did it was magic.

It was the power of laughter, Brother. Not polite nor subtle nor even terribly clever. But profound and healing laughter among old friends. Hallelujah! There's seldom enough to go around.

The Things of Summer

...in which Uncle Duke discusses some valuable tools.

Caleb is on his first baseball team this summer. I am finding this to be a most profound thing. We are communicating on a level that is almost scary for a dad and an 8 year old. He listens to what I tell him like I was in the Bigs. Now, I never actually told him that I played major league baseball. But I have not gone to any great lengths to deny it either. OK, maybe I kind of implied it. So he may be making some incorrect assumptions. Nevertheless, he listens as if I hold some valuable nuggets of baseball information. And the surprising truth is, I do. And the glory of it is, the wonder of it is, they are transferable and timeless.

He was having trouble hanging on to fly balls the other day and threw his glove down and kicked it in disgust. This triggered an immediate, almost involuntary reaction in me, like he was abusing the cat. I was in his face as soon as I could get there. "Let me explain something," I said with some force. "This glove is not some inanimate object, some old towel or sweatshirt. This glove is your friend. If you are going to play baseball, you'd better become intimate with your glove." He didn't know what the hell I was talking about, but he was paying attention. Yes, sir. He was paying attention. Kids filter out the unimportant stuff, but they know when you're serious.

I told him about buying my first glove with my father. We went together because it was a significant purchase. "I remember the way it felt. I remember the way it smelled," I told him. "I rubbed Glovolium on it once a day and pounded a ball into the pocket several thousand times a day to break it in and get the feel just right. I slept with it. I wouldn't any more kick it than I would kick my best friend. I took care of it, and it took care of me." I was apparently making some sense. His eyes were wide open, and he was looking right at me.

Like a lot of 8 year olds, Caleb has more "stuff" than I am comfortable with. For the most part he takes care of it. After a fashion. But it is just stuff, after all. And it all came pretty easily to him. I worry about whether he'll understand that things have an essence too. I worry whether he'll understand the difference between materialism and taking care of his tools, between owning a bunch of stuff and valuing your possessions. It's a subtle difference. And the Culture won't teach him. That's my job.

He doesn't have his own bat yet. We are making do for batting practice with a prehistoric looking wooden club of mine that is too heavy for him. "For Heaven's sake, go buy him a bat," his mother said. "Go buy him a bat?" I asked incredulously. "Just like that? Like a pair of socks? Like a bleeping book bag?"

Buying a bat is not some trivial purchase. There is length to consider. There is heft. There is handle size, barrel size. Most importantly, there is _feel_. Choosing a bat is like choosing a wife. It takes time. You don't just go grab one off the rack and bring it home. You pick them up one by one, wave it back and forth a couple dozen times to determine its proportions, its essence. How does it feel? Is it dependable? Reliable? How would it react with the bases loaded? These are hard questions. That's why sporting goods stores are potentially dangerous places in the Springtime.

Of course most bats are aluminum now. Aluminum bats are pretty much indestructible and are more uniform. So some of the mysticism may have gone out of the process. I never played baseball with anything other than wooden bats myself–Louisville Sluggers, blond, made of ash. Organic. Wood has a soul to it, a heart. But you can't really determine its individual character until you hit with it, until you stroke a ball and feel the way the wood responds. Some bats were really meant to be chairs or kitchen cabinets or bedposts. A select few were meant to hit baseballs. If you had a bat like that, it was OK not to let anyone use it. It was a prize possession and everyone understood. Others couldn't be trusted to take the same care. One careless swing, with the trademark not perfectly upright, could end its career. And no amount of surgery with screws and nails and tape could bring it back, though that didn't stop us from trying. Some of the most sincere tears I ever shed were in grief over a broken, trusted bat.

There is a feel to a well-struck ball with a good bat that is unlike any other experience. It is memorable. There is no vibration, no sense of hard ball meeting hard bat. The bat, as tool, cushions the hands, seemingly absorbs the ball for an instant and then sends it hurtling outward on the follow through. It is a sublime instant. Sometimes even the most solidly hit balls are caught. Many line drives become outs. But it really doesn't matter. It is a gratifying, timeless moment. A bat is still the tool that connects the boy and the ball.

It's all about respect really. I am distrustful of baseball players who break their bats intentionally. A bat ain't just a thing. A bat matters. In the same way I don't understand what kind of musician would smash his instrument. It strikes me as arrogant and disrespectful and blatantly detached. It is a failure to understand the connection. In the rush to decry a materialistic world, we have heaped all "things" and "stuff" into a pile and called them disposable, replaceable. If you break it, pitch it. If you lose it, buy another. Well things can have souls too. It is not wrong to value a thing and treat it with respect. It has to do with Zen, with awareness. In the end, your bat and your glove both matter.

Well lately, I have noticed that Caleb and his glove have become pretty much inseparable. He walks around the house pounding his mitt. He spits into it, moistens it, shapes it. The other night I found him in his bed, sleeping soundly, with his glove on. I was pretty moved. Some things, it would appear, _are_ timeless.

III

Life As We Find It

Drabo and His Four Wives

...in which Uncle Duke offers his blessing.

We were in Columbia, Mo. this past weekend for Beau's graduation. If you have time, ask me what I like about him. I will undoubtedly go into some detail.

But that is not the story here. The story is about a taxi ride. The story is about that cab driver who took me from downtown Columbia to a B&B well outside of town Saturday night. It was late and it was raining, but Drabo agreed to take me home. I was in a conversational mode and asked him how his night was going. I can't say for sure that I was interested in much beyond that. Most likely not. And I don't remember what it was that triggered the conversation about his four ex-wives. I don't think it was anything real direct. It may have been immediately tied in to how his night was going. I suspect that was the case. Four ex-wives (or four ex-husbands for that matter) would dominate the immediate consciousness of most of us if we had them. Over the course of the fare, he went into considerable detail about all four. All those marriages were divided into fairly predictable phases. Very good sex and intense love soon turned to indifference, then to contempt which eventually turned to outright malice.

The time frames for these relationships were a little vague. But Drabo still seemed like a relatively young man, so they must have been of short duration. Or perhaps there was some relationship overlap. In any case, his marital turn-around rate was pretty impressive. There couldn't have been much time in between for analysis or regret or soul-searching. These courtships had a certain fever to them. I suspect they burned pretty bright.

The way it was explained to me, the breakups had something to do with the defective personalities of all of these women and everything to do with their inability to appreciate a good thing when they had it. The climactic ruckuses would generally start in the tavern, and I got the impression that there wouldn't be many disinterested by-standers. Whole families would get involved. Sometimes there were weapons. And almost inevitably the police. They were sad stories all right, top to bottom. There were no happy endings.

He reserved particular rancor/affection for wife No. 2. "Denise was a doozie," he said. It seemed that this relationship had ended particularly badly. She had stabbed him. He had only punched her. And HE got the 18 months. The Missouri Criminal Justice System was thereafter not held in high Drabo esteem. Of all the stories, this was the saddest. I got the impression that Denise was the one who had captured and held his heart most intensely and thereafter engendered the most bitterness. Love seems to work like that. Not real Love, of course. But the kind most of us settle for.

As we got close to the B&B, he told me there was however good news on the horizon. He was dating and considering re-entering the Holy State of Matrimony. He had a feeling this was The One.

You may have noticed, the human spirit is a grand and unrelenting, indefatigable thing. It will not be restrained, no matter how much good and reliable evidence we put in front of it for reasonable restraint. Drabo certainly had a streak of optimism that ran through him. Though others would perhaps call it something else. Whatever it was, it was wide and deep.

As our friendship had not been of long duration, I did not ask a lot of the questions I wanted to ask. It seemed somewhat ungentlemanly. But I did want to ask: "Drabo, do you, by any chance, drink?" I've never seen any statistics on domestic stabbings, but my assumption is that most of them are alcohol related. So assuming that he DID drink (and this is purely an assumption on my part, other than the educated guess part of it from his repeated references to bars and taverns and his admissions about being pretty drunk for most of Marriage #4) did his drinking, or their drinking, have anything to do with the demise of any of his multiple marriages? I wasn't going to try and FIX him. I was just curious to know if the connection had ever dawned on him.

I liked him. He was a bright guy, a hard working guy. But I wanted to shake him by the shoulders and yell at him that oft-repeated aphorism: "HEY, DRABO! IF YOU DO WHAT YOU ALWAYS DID, YOU GET WHAT YOU ALWAYS GOT!!!" But at 3am, in my condition, I realized that I couldn't yell that at him without a good portion of it blowing back in my direction. None of us are very astute at that one. For example, I'd love to get rid of that inner tube around my middle. But I like chips and ice cream. A lot. And I'd love to sleep better, soundly and more consistently. But all I've ever read on the subject tells me that alcohol exacerbates that condition. And I really don't want to hear that. I like my Manhattans. And I also like a little wine with dinner. And maybe a nightcap. No, I'd rather scout around for an over-the-counter med with all the right effects and none of those annoying side-effects. So I've learned to wear bulky sweaters and live with a little less sleep. Drabo, for his part, keeps looking for The Right One, The One with whom he'll live permanently in that blissed out part of marriage. But mostly he will live alone.

So we all make choices. Change is hard, and sometimes it's just easier to accept less. I admit I did not really ask him the questions that begged to be asked. But if I had, and if he was in a state of clarity and self-awareness, I'm going to guess that he would have told me that he didn't really expect long-term happiness. It was out of his reach. Beyond his grasp. Maybe he would have told me, in a burst of honesty, that he didn't really deserve more than what he got. He was just hoping against hope that this time Phase I of his short term marriages would last forever. He just wanted the Highs, knowing he could live with the Lows. He would settle for a long shot.

Well, I said good-night, wished him luck and shook his hand. But I wanted to tell him more. I wanted to tell him that he did deserve better. And so did all those women. They didn't have to settle. I wanted to encourage some broader thinking about karma and consequences and causes and conditions and long term happiness and all that stuff that none of us want to hear about or deal with. But he had another fare waiting. And in truth, my 3am advice is rarely reliable.

So I gave him a nice tip instead. I was feeling wealthy after all, with no more college tuition to pay. I told him to consider it an early wedding present.

The Big "C"

...in which Uncle Duke examines his internal rhythms.

Having just returned from vacation, I am of course acutely aware of my own bowels. They required a fair amount of my attention while we were away. We all know the impact they can have on our daily existence and how much of our mental activity they can occupy. I kind of knew that, I think. But there's nothing like a week or so away from home to bring all that back into focus. Being Regular is *hard work*!

You see, we (and I use this word loosely—meaning, as far as I am aware, me) are creatures of habit. By and large, in our day to day lives, we get up at pretty much the same time. We eat at more or less the same time. Generally it's the same types of foods, the kinds we have grown to like. This is also, not coincidentally, the kinds of food our bacteria like and have learned to process. We follow patterns and go to bed kind of about the same time. Our bodies get in very comfortable little grooves. And we have our little elimination routines. It's hard to say whether we dictate these routines or they are imposed by our gut bacteria. We could perhaps say it is a joint decision. No matter. We all just want to feel good and be happy, after all. And when our microbiomes are happy, we are happy. When all is said and done, 100 trillion microbial cells can't be wrong. End of story.

But traveling puts a kink in our daily rituals. It interferes with our habitual sequencing. That comfortable little throne that we use every day, it is far, far away. And the ones we must use in its stead are unfamiliar, sometimes even user unfriendly. They are in in airports or service stations or restaurants, noisy hubs with people swirling about, coming and going. Some of those characters coming out of those stalls are downright unsavory, not people you'd ever want to share a taxi with, much less a toilet. Ick!

And, speaking personally, there is a certain aesthetic that my bodily rhythms require. Elimination is a contemplative act. Not at all unlike meditation. Enlightening in many ways. It is a quiet time, a time of self-examination and personal liberation. Multi-tasking is not allowed here. One assumes the position, communes with one's own inner digestive system, the small intestines aligning with the large, the abdominal muscles communicating with the sphincter, on down the line. One feels the contractions and understands intuitively the wonders of Gravity and the harmony of the Movement. It can be a beautiful experience.

But on the road, it can get complicated. Often before one can establish a real rhythm, there are impatient fellow travelers standing in line outside the stall, waiting for us to do our business, vacate and move on. Like this is some kind of timed exercise? This is not conducive to a satisfying or efficient experience. "I beg your pardon, sir. This is serious work I'm doing here. This is not a command performance. It is requires concentration and focus. If it is not done well and completely, I could DIE. No, my good man. In this case, haste does NOT make waste. Applying undo pressure only leads to a form of performance anxiety. Which serves to prolong or even block the process totally. Banging on the stall door and yelling 'Hey Sparky, you OK in there?' is not helpful."

So ambience is a necessary element of regularity (or as I like to call it, Bowel Harmonics). But another very crucial variable is diet. On vacation we tend to deviate from our normal diet. For example, in the Midwest, I seldom have oysters and Champaign for breakfast. On a Tuesday. But in Northwest Washington State, it seemed like a good idea. And in truth it was. Oysters, eggs and Champagne are a wonderfully stimulating combination and I would do it again. The problem was that my particular gut flora that typically deal with oysters and Champagne are not active in the morning. They don't generally get pressed into service until much later in the evening. And as a rule, they only work weekends. So my systems started getting a little behind at that point.

And then there was all that salmon. The Northwest is all about salmon. And I eat some salmon at home. I'll have a little salmon loaf from time to time. And I'll put some on a cracker now and again, but it's not a big part of my diet. My assumption is that my alimentary canal was temporarily overwhelmed by the profusion of salmon. The same thing happened to Lewis and Clark. I dare say my bacteria/gut flora were ill-prepared for the yeoman work they were asked to do. They were temporarily stunned by the volume. And the next thing you know, we had a Situation. The Works got gummed up. Or as my father used to say, stove up. The big "C". Not uncommon for a vacation.

There are mitigating measures one can take of course. Probiotics, supplements and some very effective over-the-counter products. But they often produce results in ill-timed fits and inconvenient starts. They sometimes work a little too well. The cure becomes worse than the ailment.

Mostly what it takes is Time and Patience. But who has time for that on vacation–when there are trails to walk and tides coming in and ferries to catch. So the Fundamentals get neglected. The Basics get postponed. And we all know that those Bodily Functions which have their own precise schedules can not be postponed. Or they can. But with predictable results.

So in the end, I very much LIKE vacations. There is something wonderful and enriching about new Vistas, new Horizons. It is a valuable experience. But there is also something to be said for the familiar, the comfortable. And this morning, as my old truck and me made it again down Highway F toward work, I began to feel that familiar grumbling and rumbling that signifies to me a system in harmony, a body in balance. A Happy System. It's good to be back. My only fear is that I may never be able to retire.

Blood Matters

...in which Uncle Duke examines his inheritance.

I think a lot about continuity these days. Forward and backward. About the strings and the genes and the traditions that bind us together. I suppose I'm in search of a legacy—one I can live with, one I can pass on. I'm not sure why. It seems important.

Looking backward, I am a child of prestige. Though not in any serious financial sense. I was born into a world of emotional affluence and unconditional support. I am the product of people who were, by all accounts, thrilled by my conception and eager to be parents. It was a world of sufficient time, maternal attention and paternal provision. It was a world that cared about me.

In our small town, we were of the aristocracy. Such as it was. Small "a". The aristocracy also included the dentist whose office was on the 2nd floor over the hardware store and the bank president who milked cows before and after bank hours. It was a town where rich men drove old pick-up trucks and women of wealth darned socks and collected soap slivers.

It was a town in which you were known. Your parents and grandparents and beyond were matters of record. "I grew up with your grandfather. He was a fine man," an older person would say. This was more than an observation, more than a compliment even. It was an implied expectation, a broad overlay of history in which you had a future place. Not reserved necessarily. But set aside. You were penciled in. Not for any specific accomplishments but in a leadership role. The pieces were in place—the genetics, the support, the surrounding discipline and direction.

Your name meant something. There were multiple generations of Haydons who had lived their lives basically with that goal in mind—to make their name stand for something. That was my inheritance. It was a tangible, marketable thing. It was collateral. You could, as they say, take it to the bank.

But that door swung both ways. It could work against you. If one of your forbearers had lived a self-centered, valueless life, if he had somehow shirked responsibility and besmirched his own name, left others in the lurch, he would have simultaneously sullied your name for generations to come. You were one of them! This phrase could be stated with some considerable distaste. Almost a spit. The shadow over your name would last much longer than the recollection of the individual or his deeds. It would affect how people looked at you, and it would probably take a lifetime of virtue and civic responsibility to climb out of that hole. God forbid if any of your people were mixed up somehow with The Law. The blemish on your name was irreversible. It was pock marked and pitted beyond restoration. There was no future here for the likes of you.

But through happenstance and shear good fortune, I am a product of generations who guarded their name religiously. And except for several profligate years in college, I have too. Not perhaps as stoutly as they. But I've tried. I have avoided ethics violations of front-page proportions and I have not appeared on any Reality TV shows. I consider these to be, in this day and time, no small accomplishment.

Yet I am not sure that it is worth what it once was. My parents stayed in the town and in the state where they were born and rooted. Their histories intertwined with the history of the county and the region. And the memory of our family's role in that development was still strong. I on the other hand have moved out into a world where family names are almost irrelevant. They are like license plates. Everyone has one, but no one pays much attention to it. The year and make of the vehicle are what's important. We must prove ourselves daily to a sea of people who really don't much care about our bloodlines. And I'm not saying that's necessarily bad. But there is strength to be derived from tradition and lineage.

Where I grew up, I saw my family name on street signs and on buildings and weekly in the paper, always as I recall, doing positive things. They were City Fathers, standard bearers. I grew up with a sense of worth which had been hand-carved by generations before me. My sons, not growing up surrounded by their genealogical past, are pretty much on their own. There're just them and their mother and me. There is not the accumulated local memory of their name.

When you move away from your history, you have to pack it up and take it with you. You stuff the corners with stories and decorate the walls with portraits and photos. Venerable, bearded old men with eyes just like your first-born's and gussied up, somber ladies with the jaw line and that fierce, determined look of your youngest.

It is important for us to know that we have a past, that we had histories that began before we were born. We are not insular packages with incidental last names. We are an accumulation of genetic bits and pieces with ancestral memories. Chances are, if you are very good at something or struggling with something else, you are not the first of your lineage with those tendencies. They made decisions based on those skills and deficiencies–some correct, some less so. There is knowledge we carry in our veins. It is a map of how to negotiate our daily paths based on our ancestors' past experiences. And it is all accessible.

I am proud of my pedigree. In the same way I am proud of my progeny. To say that I come from good people is a full bore compliment. It is to bolster my own self-opinion, generally when I most need it bolstered. To say that my family carried themselves well is to apply external starch to my own backbone at times when it could use some stiffening.

I happen to like my ancestors. I respect them. Historically, I admit they were as dysfunctional as anyone else's. I would in fact hold them up to any other family in that regard. They were by all accounts obstinate, narrow-minded and chock full of eccentricities– and, by God, proud of it.

From what I know of them though, I imagine them struggling to do the right thing. Losing multiple children in childbirth and suffering failure after failure, they evidently persevered. I feel their sorrows and their confusion on a daily basis. I imagine them dragging themselves out of bed in the morning with the dread of the immediate in their stomachs. I imagine them doing distasteful tasks, making difficult decisions, while focusing on a tiny picture of a small child, yet unborn. I imagine that it was an image of one of their descendants, one of us, waiting in line for their name and all that they intended it to stand for.

Beauty Secrets

...in which Uncle Duke examines the origins of Beauty.

I have long been a student of beautiful women. I thought I would grow out of it, but I haven't. Curiously, I do not hesitate to admit it. How could I? I married one, for Christ's sake. Nor am I ashamed of myself. It largely indicates, as far as I can tell, that I am still breathing and that my brain waves are not entirely flat. I don't think I ogle or leer, but perhaps I may occasionally tarry too long in my gaze. Though I try to be discrete, I fear that sometimes I am not. It is possible that I am in fact, at times, quite transparent in my admiration. If that is so, I am contrite. I mostly apologize. Though I'm not entirely sure why.

Beauty is a curious thing. Historically, it has led tribes and nations to war and certainly changed the course of human events time and again. The Greek and Roman gods were all susceptible to the charms of Beauty. They used it to bargain and manipulate and influence. As do we. It is bought and sold in the Marketplace. Everyday. All over the World. Often at great price. Beauty is Power. Universally, it is money in the bank.

Of course Beauty is thought of as almost exclusively feminine. It is in this area that the sexes are really not very equal. Masculine beauty has played a role from time to time in the course of things, but mostly in a minor way. Handsome will get you a few votes or sell some tickets, but it's not an everyday force like Female Beauty. Beautiful Women have doors opened for them that the rest of us are required to knock on, beat on, take tests, present resumes and pay bribes to get through. Beautiful Women are not at all like you and I.

It would be naïve to think that Beauty is not linked to sex. Of course it is. Most everything is. But Pretty in particular is. We act differently around It. We change the rules to accommodate It. This is because there is generally some faint hope of seduction in the air. Even for the oldest and lumpiest of us, there is some stray thought of sexual interaction. Even if we wouldn't. Even if we couldn't. It is a well-known fact that fantasies persist well beyond the remotest possibility of fulfillment. But mostly it is that men just enjoy being around beautiful women. They enjoy looking at and vaguely flirting with those women, however unattainable, whose bodies and features exemplify that which the culture deems desirable. I don't entirely get it. In this case, I _do it_ and I don't get it. The logic is buried in obscure parts of our animal brains.

All of this of course begs the question of what is Beauty. It seems so wound up with the roots of biology and reproduction as to be indecipherable even to us. I have read that perceived Beauty has less to do with the exceptional than the average. The fact is that we visually scan each other and look for symmetry. Our eyes and brains make subliminal measurements, calculate angles and compare values and ratios to arrive at the absolute geometric mean, which is our measure of Beauty. It turns out that Beauty is less about the exotic than the very ordinary. The most perfect symmetry is how we define health and, by extension, Beauty. It is the extreme average.

But what's so pretty about that? Well, we humans are looking for the external manifestations of internal, genetic normalcy. These angles and ratios are connected to normalcy which is related to reproductive capacity. It is thought that the typically average is attractive because the average suggests something which has adapted to its environment and is healthy. Good looks are a sign of health and of being relatively disease-free. Long, shiny hair, for example, is not intrinsically more beautiful than short hair. The preference for long, shiny hair evolved because that indicated a healthy, well-nourished body. And good teeth are important. So you get points for a nice smile. Evolution has so shaped our brains and minds that we find most beautiful those faces and bodies which are most suggestive of being suitably fit for healthy reproduction. We are attracted to what works as a species. Imagine that!

Age and experience, by the way, are not positive Beauty Factors. As a rule, they do not accentuate Beauty. Age, in fact, obscures Beauty. It wrinkles It, blurs It, dulls It. Facial asymmetry tends to increase with age, as does sagging and bagging, stooping and drooping. The natural attractors diminish. Read 'em and weep.

But in procreative logic, this makes perfect sense. Younger women are more likely to conceive and bear healthy young and survive the experience. Of course youth has the advantage. The link between Beauty and Sexual Reproduction is still a short one, even though we have been de-linked from the pressures of procreation for hundreds of generations. We are hard-wired, biologically determined, to ensure the survival of the species. At the end of the day, our primitive, furry brains are still looking for partners to breed with.

But some elements of Beauty are highly variable. They vary from age to age and culture to culture. It used to be for example that heft was beautiful. When we struggled seriously for food, women with meat on their bones were considered more desirable since they were more successful somehow in the skill of acquiring and consuming food. Padded hips and thunder thighs were serious attractors. Woo-hoo! In other ages, when almost all of us were peasant farmers, women with pale skin were in the minority. They were considered attractive since it meant that they were successful enough to have avoided lives of menial labor. Now of course, thin and tanned are the standards. They are indicators of the current marker for success– ceaseless self-absorption.

In the present world, it strikes me that Beauty, real and apparent, has never been more paramount. An incredible amount of time, attention and money are devoted to the end-purpose of making women more attractive. Or less old. In the United States, more money is spent on Beauty than on education or social services. And that's not counting laser technology, microsurgery and injection therapy. From toenails to highlights, women buff and polish themselves for the purpose of being noticed.

This is not to say that men are not conscious of their own looks. They are indeed. They struggle mightily to keep their hair, and they fuel a highly profitable steroid trade to get those real showy abs. But if you look at the numbers, men are just not in the same cosmetic league. And a casual look around most any mixed-use bathroom will quickly verify that. A little aftershave goes a long way.

Nope. No question. In this department, Women Rule. And further, unless I'm mistaken, the trend is to outline, accentuate, boost and generally expose the female form. From a very early age. My research is incomplete and based solely on visual investigation, but I'd say there are more square centimeters of exposed female flesh today than at any point in recorded history–going back to the point at which we began to wear any clothes at all. No wonder Muslims are mad. While boys' shorts are pretty much indistinguishable from long pants, women's shorts have gotten teenier. Necklines on everyday wear go south while engineering innovations and light-weight alloys push and nudge and crowd the female breast well into the Northern Hemisphere. And some exposed midriff is now de rigueur. Belly buttons are objects of ornamentation, ringed and tattooed. Even ankles and toes are bangled and bejeweled. Yowza! There's sure plenty to look at.

Understand, this is not a trend I necessarily oppose. *Au contraire.* It's a wonderful time to be alive. As trends go, I pay attention to this one. Let it be known that I support the undraping and decoration of the female form in everyday fashion.

Though as a student of the Art Form, I must say I am suspicious of it. As I generally am of that which is vanity-driven. There are aspects of the Beauty Game which are disturbing. Primarily I suppose because it is dishonest and promotes shallow attention, which we, on most levels, profess to abhor. Although it is true that Beauty is Power, it is often False and it's always Temporary. There are elements of the old bait-and-switch here. Deception is a tool used to influence the outcome.

But that shouldn't be too surprising. That's really the way it's always been. Nature has always used trickery for its own singular purpose. Which is Survival. Which ultimately involves Procreation. Which is intrinsically bound up with the attraction of Beauty–or the perception of It. Ah, what a wonderfully woven web is this World. Caveat emptor, I say. Caveat emptor.

A Hard Look at Christmas

…in which Uncle Duke recalls the Newton sisters.

I don't know why, but I started thinking about the Newton sisters the other day. Miss Piety and Miss Chastity. They owned a little grocery store on the corner of Walnut and High St. Neither had ever married, and they lived together above the store.

I guess the reason I was thinking about them was that I was remembering my father's Christmas rounds. See every year, a week or so before Christmas, Daddy would make up a bunch of Christmas baskets and take them around to some of his friends and relatives and customers. Most every year I'd go with him.

My father was a thoughtful man, but not what you'd call an extravagant one. He was also generous, but not hardly to a fault. A couple of World Wars and a Depression had convinced him to hang on to his nickels pretty good. So he always gave everybody fruit and nuts. That was what Christmas was for him on the farm—fruit and nuts. It may not have been lavish. But it was, by God, Christmas.

Anyway, we'd bundle up those grapefruits and oranges and Brazil nuts and pecans and apples and cashews and bed them in some green crinkly paper and tie a big red ribbon on the handle. Then we'd take them around to the folks on his list. The list wasn't that long, and I think everyone knew they were being honored. Everyone, that is, except the Sims sisters.

They were never very impressed and made no attempts to pretend they were. And this even though Daddy every year saved Piety and Chastity til last and always put something extra in their basket. He'd always tuck a pint of Heaven Hill sipping whiskey underneath all the fruit and nuts and green paper. Now no one in that town ever accused the Newton sisters of being untrue to their names. They were certainly pious and chaste enough to suit just about anybody. It is also true however that neither of them was named Sobriety. They did enjoy their toddies. But you'd have never known it by their reaction. We never got any elaborate "thank you's" or "Aw, you shouldn't have's" from either of them. It didn't seem to bother Daddy. But boy, it made me mad.

They were plain mean is the way I saw it. They were old and they were ugly and they were mean. And I never could figure out why Daddy year after year persisted in trying to be nice to them. Finally I broke down and asked him.

"I understand why you'd think they're mean," he said. "I did too. But they're not. They like to act like it, but they're not. You probably think they never smile either. I got to admit it ain't real obvious, but they do. You just got to look hard to see it."

"Like today," he added, "when I gave Miss Piety–she's the one with the mole–the basket. And she asked: 'Is this all? You gave us more last year.' She was smiling. You got to look hard in the corners of their eyes. They're laughing. In their fashion they're guffawing. They're slapping their knees and hoo-hawing to beat the band. They just don't show it like most folks. No, they're fine ladies. It hasn't been easy on them in this town. You just got to look harder in some folks. You'll see that some day."

Well the next time I was in their store examining the baseball cards, scrutinizing the packages, holding them up to the light, trying actually to peer through the paper at the cards inside to see if they were ones I wanted, Miss Chastity came up behind me. She was the one with the mustache. "You looking for something in particular," she asked. "We got a x-ray machine in the back if you need one." I thought she might be kidding, but she sure didn't look like it. I looked at her real hard. I looked right into her steely eyes. I stared as long as I could at their wrinkled old corners. I zoomed in hard to see if there was any hoo-hawing going on in there, any mirth of any kind.

And you know what? There wasn't a bit of humor there. Not one damn drop. There wasn't even a smirk that I could see. Never ever did either. Daddy's could just see something I couldn't, I reckon.

Well I'm not sure why I started thinking about the Newton sisters. They're part of a world gone by, cold and buried. It could be the time of year, I suppose. December's long nights tends to bring back images and faces from other times that we've let go. But anyway, the other day, here came Miss Piety and Miss Chastity, uninvited, floating back through my sub-conscious–their faces just so clear. They were still way ugly. The years hadn't improved their looks. But, the strange thing was, they were smiling. Not much. Hardly at all. Just enough so I could notice.

Art, Life and Stuff

…in which Uncle Duke ingeniously explains the title.

I have always admired Art Teachers. There is something pure there, something uncluttered. I have respect for all teachers actually, but classroom teachers are tied to a lot of facts, dates and theorems. They are connected to the known world in a way which can be burdensome. They have bags of information which they must hand out. And it is their job, they are judged by how well their students give it back to them in the same form that they hand it out.

Art is different. There are no right answers, no wrong answers. It is in fact a lot like life in that regard. Which is why it is so little respected in the culture. It is too hard to define, not quantifiable, difficult to test and grade. For that reason, among others, kids who are poor students in the regular classroom can often excel at art. Those who don't read well sometimes combine shapes and colors in wonderful ways. Those who don't fit in socially can lose themselves in worlds of paint and clay. It is a level field of imagination on which those who look at the world differently can excel.

My friend David Lee is an Art Teacher. We grew up together in my little town. And from the very beginning, it was apparent that David Lee was an artist. I had some artistic inclinations my own self, but I managed to obscure them pretty well. David Lee apparently didn't have that option.

It is not easy being an artist in a little town. There are ways of doing things which have been accepted for generations. Those who run counter to the prevailing culture are often seen as perversions of the natural order. And artists tend to do things which go against the grain.

As a for instance, David Lee had to cut the grass when he was a kid, just like we all did. But he didn't do it like the rest of us. We all started on the outside and worked our way in, in nice little symmetric, decreasing rectangles. Or back and forth in rows–the way the civilized world has always cut grass, the way God Hisownself intended it. David Lee would just pick a spot and wade in. He'd start cutting spirals or parabolas or triangles, right out of the middle. He'd mow for a while and then he'd go up to his room and look at it. Sometimes he'd let it get good and high and do kind of a maze thing, what you could call a labyrinth. Sometimes he'd write obscene words and other irreverent stuff you could only read from his room. Once he did a reasonable likeness of Sr. Agnes Marie. Life was just a big canvas for David Lee.

They had a big yard in the center of town, and this didn't go unnoticed. As I said, it is a dangerous thing to go against established standard procedure in a small town. It wasn't long before David Lee had a nickname. He became "Swirl", as in "he cut a big old swirl out of the middle of his yard!" And the thing about nicknames in a small town is that pretty quick they become permanent. An unfortunate quirk in the 3rd grade will follow you around for a lifetime and wind up on your headstone. So "Swirl" he remains. Originally it was not a complimentary nickname. But over the years he has acquired some begrudged respect. Primarily I suppose because he wasn't ashamed of his tendencies, nor even embarrassed. He was An Artist. And he didn't mind who knew. That kind of honesty, over time, will get you respect.

It's kind of a long, winding story, but David Lee went away to college. He taught in Louisville for a while but eventually came back and is now The Art Teacher in the local school. He is responsible for the artistic development of 750 kids. And by extension, the whole town really. It is a responsibility that he takes very seriously. He is a valued member of the community and recently built a house there. It is a pretty unassuming little frame home on the outskirts of town. From the outside you wouldn't know it was The Art Teacher's house except that the shutters are all different colors and the lawn is a little odd. The inside is a different matter though. David Lee considers concealed wiring and plumbing to be hypocritical, dishonest, like we're ashamed of our inner workings. In his house, the infrastructure is the exo-structure. The pipes and wires are on the outside of the walls. He has them painted different colors with vines growing up the water pipes and what looks kind of like cave paintings on the duct work. He had to pay extra for it, but the effect is pretty extraordinary. There's sure plenty to look at.

As The Art Teacher, David Lee has a tendency to latch on to troubled souls. Sherman is just such a soul. Large and disruptive, they've been trying to figure out what to do with him for years. Now in the 7th grade, he's pretty much raising himself. And not doing a very good job of it. He can barely read and passes into the next grade every year only because of a lack of acceptable alternatives. He has however shown some fascination with art. Even some aptitude. He combines materials in curious ways, ways no one else would think of. It doesn't always work, but it at least indicates that there is thought going on in there. This is not always terribly obvious.

David Lee has been working with him on his class project. Sherman had an idea for a piece combining braised copper and modeling clay. They had started on it earlier in the year, but supervising Sherman is a lot more work than doing it yourself. He is not terribly dependable, nor always open to suggestion. Frankly, David Lee's patience and energy had run thin. There were in fact 749 other artistic souls to shepherd. But he did want Sherman to finish the project and had been applying some considerable pressure to that end.

On the day of the deadline, the projects rolled in. There were watercolors, acrylics, mosaics. There was paper mache, carved balsa wood, baked clay and stretched fabric–some very good and some schlepped together. But in each of them, he could see some considerable parental involvement. With his trained eye, he could see some bracing and structural blocking and polishing that wouldn't have been there without some adult supervision. Which was fine. Art is after all a community project. In the end it is about cooperation.

That morning, David Lee caught sight of Sherman skulking out the door. He called to him. When he didn't respond, he hustled after him and caught up with him in front of his locker. "Where's your project, Sherman?" His posture was stiff. Sherman was braced, defiant and ready for a fight. "I don't got a project." David Lee leaned in. He was angry himself now. He began to talk to him about responsibility and deadlines and grades. His finger was in Sherman's chest. Suddenly, Sherman spun around and flung open his locker door. Inside, on the floor of the locker, was a jumble of copper and clay, on an irregular base of 2x4's with bent nails sticking out. Sherman trembled in the middle of the hall, standing in the midst of his own humiliation and frustration. "There's my stupid project. I tried," he yelled. "It didn't work. It sucks." He began to sob loudly.

David Lee reached out for him and put his arms around him. He could feel the strength of his anger. He held him hard for a long time. As he did, he looked over Sherman's shoulder at the piece. He had to admit that Sherman had critiqued his own work pretty well. It did suck. It was a mess. Still, it was unique. There were the beginnings of shape and form. There was evidence of some imagination and thought. It could work. With some combined effort, some adult assistance, they could still maybe make the deadline.

That's the thing about art. It's not always a product. It's not always an award winner. It's more about process. There is an idea, some conflict and sometimes even resolution. It's a lot like life. It's a lot like Sherman. You never know how it's going to turn out.

The Buddha in the Buzzard

...in which Uncle Duke heaps praise on the much maligned buzzard.

I find lately that I am wildly envious of turkey vultures. More so this Spring than ever. I suppose it comes from watching them soar effortlessly hundreds of feet above me. I am struck by the view they must have. With their six-foot wings fully extended, they ride thermals above breathtaking landscapes. With imperceptible shifts in the tips of their wings, they change directions, elevate, descend, stall, dive and float. While I am deeply rooted amidst bad news and deteriorating conditions of all sorts, the vulture soars above me in this great limitless, placid place. Where they are, the World must make more sense. I realized I had sorely missed them over the Winter.

They migrated back again this year–on the Vernal Equinox. The exact day. Just like last year. And the year before. They went back to the same communal roost. Most of them to the same tree. The same limb. Predictable and dependable. I like that in a scavenger.

They are certainly curious birds. Enigmatic. Close relatives of the exalted California condor, the vulture is generally reviled. Though certainly not the most handsome of creatures, they are perhaps one of the more elegant. Their reputation as vile and repugnant harbingers of the dead and the unclean belies the fact that they are fastidious, even dapper in their habits. By all accounts, they bathe often, submersing in ponds, shaking and scrubbing for half an hour. Then they walk up on the bank and hold their wings out to dry in the sun. They spend a minimum of two to three hours a day preening. That's beyond hygiene. In my book, that borders on vanity. I bet if they had mirrors, it would be four to six hours. They'd be teen-agers. Who knew?

Many humans are appalled by their eating habits. Abhorrent, loathsome creatures, they are called. And I admit that they eat a lot of dead animal. But so do we. And we pay dearly for ours. Vultures pay nothing at all for theirs. And ours have probably been dead longer. Granted, our dead animals have been kept in a somewhat cleaner environment, at a more controlled temperature probably. But still...I consider this a fine distinction.

They have found a food source that is both free and plentiful. I suspect we're just jealous.

Turkey buzzards perform a valuable environmental service, taking care of matter that is a breeding ground for pathogens harmful to most species. But not harmful to them. No way. Anthrax? They laugh at anthrax. They eat it like popcorn shrimp. Rabies? 'Yum-yum.' Cholera? 'H-m-mm…an interesting aftertaste.' Vultures are protected from diseases associated with decaying animals by a very sophisticated immune system. Their digestive system has the unique ability to kill any virus and bacteria in the food it eats. Even their bodies are immune. Bacteria die on their faces. Whoa! Of fear probably. Great God, what a creature!

My mother used to tell me that I had the gastrointestinal system of a turkey buzzard. As I look back on it, I don't think she really meant it as a compliment. But I took it as one. Even then, I was honored to be compared with this spectacular beast whose scientific name, *Cathartes Aura*, means "cleansing breeze". Who wouldn't die for a moniker like that? Walk down the street, "Yo! Cleansing Breeze. Whazzup, C.B.?" How cool would that be!

While it is technically true that others' misfortune is their good fortune, they are not embarrassed by the grisly nature of their jobs. To the contrary, they take a great deal of pride in the efficiency with which they perform it. They are highly evolved, remarkable specialists. For example, they have over time rid their heads of feathers so they can thrust themselves into the gut of a carcass without leaving a nasty, hard-to-clean mess. **Clever!** They release urine down their legs to clean off bacteria. **Ingenious!!** They defend themselves by projectile vomiting, hurling ingested remains at potential attackers. ***Brilliant!!!*** The much-maligned buzzard is the ultimate martial artist. He of so little respect is a Zen Master of aggressive self-defense. I love irony.

And they seem to be thriving. I see them in increasing numbers, populating the skies. What with the number of cars and trucks out there, there's a lot of road kill, baking on the asphalt. With the scarcity of predators, there're a lot of animals dying of old age. A lot of unclaimed carcasses. With all the old coon hunters dying off, there's a lot of carrion out there for the taking. I doubt that the Earth has ever been so bountiful a place for a scavenger. These days, in this part of the world, it is good to be a buzzard.

By all accounts they are extremely inquisitive and intelligent. They possess a certain wry wit. And why wouldn't they? Any animal that can ascend to those heights and remain there as a silent observer for hours at a time would have a distinct advantage over the rest of us who struggle along, eyeball-to-eyeball with our peers and our dirty laundry and the rest of our earth-based problems. The vulture transcends the hubbub and rises above the din, gracefully soaring on the Earth's good will and abundance. Where they go, there is only the Music of the Wind. Up there, you can listen to the Sound of the Universe. Way up there, you can hear the Voice of God.

I like to think that if I had that type of access, that type of perspective on a regular basis, once a day, once a month even, I would be much wiser than I am now. Those of us who are earth-bound are almost 2-dimensional in perspective. Up and down is a limited option. We are ruled by Gravity. If you're a buzzard, Gravity ain't such a big deal.

So vultures have a much broader vision, a more expanded view of the world around them. Time and space would be different from that altitude. It's always seemed to me that if we could stretch out our arms like that and be lifted by warm air, if we could extend our fingers and feel the differences in pressure, we could learn to play the wind like a harpsichord and turn Energy into Art. If we could roll with the wind, float with the clouds and waltz across the sky, we could see the bemused Face of Creation in the landscape below. If we could understand the Seasons, know the days without a calendar, Time without a watch, we could touch the Eternal. If we could feel the Poles and understand the Cycles like the lowly vulture, we would be enlightened bearers of Truth and Balance. We would be the smiling Buddha-bird. We could be the Cleansing Breeze. How cool would that be?

Blood Sports

...in which Uncle Duke goes one-on-one with ticks.

I have this thing going with ticks. The deal is that I enter into their space on a fairly regular basis, and they try to make a meal out of me. I actually do not object to this. Blood-sucking parasites have to eat too. They don't eat much, and I am warm blooded and a pretty tasty, tick morsel, if I do say so myself.

What it's about is an individual case of survival-of-the-fittest in which I am trying to resist becoming the victim. It is the age-old story–the Hunter and the Hunted. In this case I am the Hunted. It is a friendly competition that has become not-so-friendly. This summer, it has become...personal. This is now...Mano-a-Ticko!

The tick is a more than worthy adversary, to be sure. It patiently lies in wait in bushes and trees for what Biologists euphemistically call "hosts"–you, me, dogs, deer, possum. It is particularly sensitive to movement and carbon dioxide, signals that a host may be near. Their grasping forelegs allow them to climb on and quickly find a protected spot. They're faster than they look. The little buggers can motor when they want. And their crablike legs and a sticky secretion help hold the tick to its host. They then sink their specialized mouthparts into the flesh, inject a little anticoagulant and begin to feed. When they are full, when they are gorged in blood, they drop off. In truth, they are amazingly efficient little feeding machines and are well-represented all over the world. But for all their efficiency, they do not get much respect. They are in fact feared, vilified, defiled and despised.

Well I have all the respect in the world for this humble, little prick of an arachnid. But I confess they are becoming a considerable annoyance to me. I am spending more and more of my time detaching them from my nether parts, and I admit to measurable resentment. Blasphemy and high invective have been ineffective thus far, and my threats are admittedly empty. I adamantly refuse to wear long sleeve shirts all summer, or to duct tape my cuffs, or to stay out of the woods. And I steadfastly refuse to use any stinking sprays.

Historically, my general strategy in these cases has always been to evolve. Change per se, which is to say changing my own behavior, is not my strong suit. That requires a certain mental dexterity that I've never mastered. Additionally, I do not make concessions well, even when faced with troublesome facts. In short, I change with considerable resistance and very little grace. However, I can tolerate discomfort for long periods of time. This, coupled with my natural inclination to obstinacy, has required my physiological self to evolve pretty quickly and effectively.

For example, mosquitoes don't bother me much. They used to. Oh, my! They would buzz around my ears all night and suck on my knuckles and toes at will. They were a tremendous source of aggravation and I would flail away at them and curse them and their Maker on a pretty regular basis. But I never conceded to those mosquito repellants or bug sprays. No Sir! All that stuff was just one more thing to lug along on the camping trip and clutter up closets the rest of the time. And I hate those yuppie insect candles. They are designed to be used once or twice and then accumulate in one's basement. And besides, to my mind, they are beacons to the insect world, advertising ankles and elbows to be nibbled. Protein by the pound, they proclaim. They only inflame mosquito blood lust if you ask me.

Anyway, I've always preferred to curse the darkness rather than light one mosquito coil. Evolve or Die, I swore. And to be honest, there were some rough days and nights in there. But by refusing all those applied, external defense systems, my body was forced to resort to Plan B–The Interior Defense System. I am not exactly sure how it works (I am not always privy to my body's inner workings. It does not care to worry me with such things.) but I'm pretty sure that I have ingeniously evolved to either smell bad or taste bad to mosquitoes. Maybe both. The end result is they just don't mess with me much anymore. They choose others. And if they do bite me, it doesn't itch. So I deduce that I have somehow developed an immunity to mosquito saliva. What normally takes 100s, even 1000s of generations, I've managed to accomplish in not-even one. I'm quite proud actually.

This happens all the time in the natural world. In response to predatory pressures, chemicals combine to provide a natural defense strategy. Organisms change. This only proves what I've believed for a long time. As an organism, I am pretty smart. As an organism, I make a lot of quick and pretty snappy decisions. If my brain gets involved, there are limitations. I tend to overcomplicate things, and certain restrictions may indeed apply. But as a biological entity, as an organism operating on instincts, I hold I'm pretty gosh-darned shrewd.

With some other critters however, my alternate long-term strategy has been to negotiate. I long ago made my peace with snakes and spiders. In the snake pact, I promised to remove any of their brethren from the asphalt where they had been flattened and mangled. Out of respect. Snakes in particular do not like their dead defiled like that. And they are ill-equipped to operate a scoop shovel. The snakes for their part agreed to address me as "Sir" and not sneak up on me unawares. It is a workable arrangement. I have never been bitten by a snake that I didn't deserve it.

As for spiders, I try to learn their Proper Names and give their webs a wide berth. It's not easy spinning all that silk and weaving it into such grand art. In the world I am familiar with, form and function seldom merge with such beauty. I am an ardent admirer of their work and desire only to leave it the way I found it. For three summers I have shared a workspace with, at last count, five generations of *Argiopes*, the big black and gold ones. I sidestep their webs and feed them grasshoppers (for whom I have little affinity) when times are lean. They are a handsome family, for sure. Appreciative and very courteous too. They wouldn't waste their venom on me.

Even poison oak is open to negotiation and accord. Several years ago I cut a deal with it. I promised to show it respect and not hack it or whack it or shoot it with poisons just because it was there. In return, it would not penalize me for inadvertent brushes or incidental contact. It's really just a little overly defensive and self-protective by nature. I can relate actually. Thus far, we have both been good to our word. It's an agreement we both live with rather well, I think.

Chiggers don't much bother me anymore either. Though I can't claim much credit there. Since you can't really see them, dialogue is limited. And I'm not sure what I could offer them anyway. I think I just got old and stringy, too tough to eat. Chiggers like easy, tender meals, and I'm mostly not that.

But getting back to my duel with ticks, I have not been able to strike a deal with them. And my ability to adapt to this particular predator is seriously in question. (I am apparently a prodigious CO_2 emitter.) But I will reluctantly admit that they helped bring about the brightest and shiniest moment of my entire parenting experience. I owe them, it turns out, for a bonding moment between myself and my sons which, though it happened many years ago, is burned into my memory for good.

To begin though, let me say that I admit to being proud of my primate genes. Indeed I still cling darkly to them. I actually like roots and berries. And the thought of eating grubs is not at all disgusting to me. With a little Worcestershire Sauce maybe.

So it was the pinnacle of my primate career those years ago. There I was, lying on the bed in my underwear, with my male heirs, my off-springs, my young primate men, grooming me, combing through my body hair, picking the ticks out. I was the Alpha Male, being preened by his loyal progeny. I was the Patriarch, Grand Ruler of the Territory, the Master of the Realm, the Lord of the Manor, the King with his Princes. I have never felt so honored, so revered. For an old primate, that was as good as it could get.

Diana was less thrilled. She was not born into gentility by any means. No Blue Blood, she. But being surrounded day in and day out by three farting, belching, grunting, butt-scratching males was apparently not what she had in mind at the altar. It had taken its toll over time and dulled her sense of humor some. The fact that her bed was being used as a tick staging area put her over the top. Tick picking, it turns out, was beyond the pale, and she could not be consoled. So we did not continue this ritual, though it seemed to make a good deal of sense. Harmony at home is indeed worth a lot.

But it is filed away in the old memory bank. A treasured primate moment. It is true what they say. The family that grooms together, stays together.

Home Churching

...in which Uncle Duke climbs into the pulpit.

Caleb was about nine I think when he asked why we didn't go to church. As I recall, I gave him one of my rambling answers, designed mainly to obfuscate and stall. There was some history in there, I believe–both ecclesiastical and secular. There was a smattering of politics, no doubt. Some personal sociology. And probably some other stuff I just made up on the spot. I think I told him he was being home-churched. My recollection is that it didn't really satisfy either of us, but it bought me some time to develop a proper response.

It was a moment I was largely unprepared for. It was a moment I had in fact been dreading. It was the call to task for my children's formal religious training, or lack thereof. It was guilt incarnate, knocking on the door. It was the overwhelming sense that I was a poor provider of my children's needs, that I was not giving them something that I had myself been given. It was my deeply religious forbearers reproaching me from the grave. What was the form? Where was the structure? What was the content? Where, for God's sake, was the ritual?

My own religious upbringing had been full of form and structure. Every time those church bells rang, there were specific prayers to be said. Mornings had prayers. Meals of course did. And bedtime had a long list of them. The year was in fact full of holy days of obligation and prescribed prayer.

And for sure there was plenty of ritual. There were Midnight Masses and Sunrise Services. There were feast days and organized ceremonies, with formal processions and full choirs, incense and hundreds of candles. There were sacred days of penance and fasting, of ashes and breast-beating and dark vestments. And there were days of jubilation and triumph, of strewn flowers and bright violet raiments. The rubrics prescribed all this. And we followed them to the letter. Year in and year out. Generation upon generation.

As a little parochial kid, it fit my needs well. I loved the ritual. In church, there was a time to stand up, a time to sit down, and a time to kneel down. And I knew when those times were. There was power in knowing the rules. As an altar boy, you were kind of an apprentice priest. You had to understand the timing and the order of the ritual. The priest would say this, the server would respond thusly. When he went here and did this, you went there and did that. You rang the bells at the specific time. It was all prescribed and very orderly.

And I liked order. I liked having all the answers in one book. The Baltimore Catechism answered every single question I had, and I accepted those versions of Life and Death, Heaven and Hell, the Light and the Way contained therein. I had my own personal Guardian Angel and no inclination to doubt any of it. And the knowledge that I belonged to the One, True Religion was very comforting. If you're going to belong to a religion, it might as well be the One that is Right and not any of the other ones that are Wrong. It was a secure and dandy way to grow up. And since we were all named for saints, we all essentially had two birthdays every year. That was cool.

Well, there is certainly comfort in ritual. Especially at an early age. We are a species that thrives on it and in some sense requires it. It's what we do. And, by extension, it's what we are in many ways. Additionally, there is an argument that, in parenting, form and structure are essential. They're like scaffolding. You give your children the super-structure, and later they can drape it with the whole cloth of their own theology and/or spiritual identity. I couldn't deny that I had benefited from my own.

So we began to hunt for a church. We began a Sunday search for our own religious niche. We sampled from the fare of large, steepled churches and modern, low-slung churches. We listened to bombastic preachers and humble, earnest ministers. We offered the sign of peace in progressive churches and put money in the collection basket in big, old historic churches with leaky roofs. We suffered through long-winded monologues by Direct Emissaries of the Father and sailed through mercifully short services from Friends of His Children.

I will admit that we limited ourselves to the Christian faiths. This was not out of any strong conviction, but mostly out of habit. As an analogy, it's not likely that I would, at this stage of my life, abandon baseball and become a cricket fan. I don't understand the rules. I don't know the stories or the legends. Well, I only know the Jesus legend and the stories of the Saints. Further, I'm not sure anybody else's religion has Angels. I like Angels. And I didn't know when to stand up and sit down anywhere else. So Christian it had to be.

Even in this New Testament framework however, we avoided the ones where they handled snakes or were prone to testify and speak in tongues. Although I'm sure the services are very entertaining and even spiritually uplifting in certain circumstances, I generally prefer my performance art on Saturday nights, not Sunday mornings. I get confused otherwise.

On the whole though, our sampling was, by my standards, broad and fair. It was, as they say, all good information. They all seemed very sincere and earnest and happy to share their Good News. The path to the Garden passed through their church, they all seemed to say. And they beckoned us to follow.

And I tried. I swear I did. I tried to open my head to the Message and let my heart be moved by the Spirit. I wanted to receive the blessing and accept the comfort. But in the end, I could not. I wanted it to make sense; but no matter how hard I wanted it to, it just didn't.

There were several stumbling blocks. First of all, I could not get beyond this perceived special relationship between God and the Human Race. Most everything of significance had apparently taken place within the last 3000 years or so. That enormous expanse of time which preceded (14 billion years or so by most intelligent accounting) was not of much consequence. Continents drifted apart, mountains rose and fell, species came and went, whole cultures prospered and died out. But then **We** came along. Born by peculiar happenstance in this particular time and place, **We** somehow became God's Special Project. **We** became the creatures He loved above all others in His Creation. **We** are "in His image and likeness", they say—the center of His focus and the epicenter of His Universe. In addition, **We** were somehow granted dominion over the Earth, all its Creatures and apparently anything else that strikes our fancy—the moon and the stars included, if we can ever find a way to get there.

It just struck me as arrogant. Then and now. It is the way children think of the World, with themselves at the Center of it, with all the Universe spinning around them and dependent on them. I'm sure every squirrel and bush rat thinks the same way, with the absolute, innocent arrogance that is perhaps the Ultimate Definition of Life itself. It is, in my view, a limited vision. It is a story with a questionable beginning, a present with insufficient past.

Additionally, it's always seemed to me that Organized Religions were formed, in large part, to provide mandated rules of conduct. People are, as a rule, a rough lot. Hard to control, particularly in large numbers. Laws, Legal Systems and Policing Agencies only work when they catch you–or deter you because you think you'll get caught. So Churches, Religions, were established to give us a reason to do the right thing, or, more precisely, a reason not to do the wrong thing, not to live absolutely selfishly as we are apparently inclined. We were commanded not to sin because it offended God. It hurt our Lord. And the Bearded One, the Watchful One, who stood over us 24/7 and saw all that we did and knew all that we thought, would be displeased with us. He was like the Super Computer that not only knew where we went on the Internet, but knew where we would go if no one was looking. He was like Santa Claus–all year long. And He took points away or awarded points (Naughty or Nice points) based on the teachings of the particular church or sect that we were following. The carrot was that those with enough points were allowed Eternal Happiness. The stinger was that the rest got smoked. This varied widely by geographical location, historical era and political orientation. Some restrictions did indeed apply. And dispensations, it turned out, were available.

The message was that we are sinful lowlifes that only an infinitely merciful God could love. This never rang true for me. And does not still. It seems to me that if we reverse the message, if we regard ourselves as principled creatures in a unified world, then sins against others become sins against ourselves. A lack of discipline effects our own happiness. The Seven Deadly Vices are after all crimes we perpetrate against ourselves. Our body is a temple and all that. If we have a larger and grander vision of ourselves, causing pain would be a source of personal pain. If we see it clearly, and if we value ourselves, cruelty would violate our own inner, ethical code. God is not the pained recipient of our misconduct. We are.

Finally, I confess I am wary of religions that have their own personal manual, the transcribed and immutable Word of God. I am distrustful of those who rely on this Rule Book and seek all their answers there. It is all too easily abused. Sooner or later, someone will bring out that Rule Book and bash you repeatedly over the head with it. It is the nature of Rule Books and Those Who Rigidly Live By Them. Both recent and historical events have shown us that. It is no way to run a world.

◆ ◆ ◆

So Caleb, I'd like another shot at it. It's taken me close to twenty years, but that's really about my normal response time. Here is why we don't go to church.

What I wanted from religion was help in giving you the sense that you are a fine and decent soul, in your own regard. Somehow, that's happened without formal religion. I am satisfied your mind is clear and your heart is good. Your conscience is intact, your values well defined.

Religions have always created stories to explain the unexplainable. They simplify creation and existence for the benefit of those of us with short attention spans. They are a single-source provider of answers to mysteries and dispensers of antidotes to the World's sorrow and sadness. I fear that they may sometimes get in the way of serious analysis.

And I decided that it was not my job to give you pat little answers to very complex cosmological and theological questions—or to see to it that others did. It was not my job to give you something to fear—there are natural consequences aplenty out there for that. It was not my job to close and seal the fearsome doors and to create a comfortable religious cocoon for you. It was my job though to ask you questions for which I have no answers. And let the questions lie there.

There were and are thousands of reasons out there to separate you and your brother from other people, from the rest of the World. What you call your God and how you worship Him is perhaps the most divisive one. It should unify us, but somehow it never has. So, in the end, I trusted you to create your own stories. I trusted you to find your own Answers, your own version of the Truth. Time will tell, eh. Godspeed.

Deflower Power

...in which Uncle Duke examines Virginity.

It seems like I have heard an awful lot about virgins this Century. Although it appears to vary widely from culture to culture, it is obvious that they are highly prized commodities. They are valued resources and the figurative carrots to lead men on. But, to be honest, I'm not sure I understand what the big deal is.

Speaking as someone who's never had one, I guess I don't understand the allure. The intrinsic value of "having" a virgin escapes me. There is something to penetrate, I gather–a resistant threshold to cross, some sort of thin membrane. It sounds like kind of a messy deal to me. My guess is that these first encounters are not, as a rule, terribly successful or satisfying. They would be awkward adventures at best, often ending in tears and frustration. My theory is that we're not talking about some rare, ecstatic sexual event here. It may be life defining, but it is positively not the inherent excitement of the act itself that sets its value. We are talking pure symbolism here.

I recall from my more innocent parochial days that there was some assumption that a bride would be virginal–chaste, pure, virtuous, unviolated. I always thought that was why wedding dresses were all white, and why weddings themselves were so bride-centered. There was that long, all-eyes-upon-the-bride walk down the center isle, the father escorting, with the beneficiary of all that virtue waiting at the altar. It was the symbolic passageway between innocence and womanhood.

There was, by the way, an equal and opposite assumption. That was that we, the prospective grooms, would not be chaste, pure or even virtuous. The expectation I recall was that we would be screwed, tattooed and violated up one side and down the other well before our wedding day. We owed it to ourselves. And our brides for that matter. If we were to usher them into conjugal bliss, we'd need extensive experience with multiple terribly loose women. The initiated carried the uninitiated across the threshold. That was The Rule.

The Blessed Virgin was obviously the Patron Saint and Ultimate Role

Model for virgins on this side of the World. She gave birth without having to be "violated" by man. She was "visited" by the Holy Spirit. (In sexual discussion, I've noticed that euphemisms abound.) I don't mean to argue with the Divine, but I've never understood why this was necessary. Joseph seemed a decent bloke. Why not him? The answer of course was that, given the Church's simultaneous affection for virginity and Its staunch enthusiasm for procreation, it was the best of both worlds.

On the other side of the World, the Koran apparently holds whole passels of virgins out to holy warriors as rewards for martyrdom in defending the faith. The exact number seems to vary, but it is generally more than a dozen and less than a gross. It's a significant number.

For purposes of argument, let's say that the designated number is 30. Now, my understanding is that virginity is not a renewable resource. It is a one-time condition. So 30 days later (or a Celestial Month, whichever comes first) you are left with 30 non-virgins and an Eternity still looming in front of you. What to do, what to do?

Or perhaps these virgins are redeemable? In the Afterlife, maybe you can recycle your virgins. If that's the case, however, what's the value of 30? Or a gross for that matter? Why not just get them one at a time? Or two by two? This lump sum payment is inefficient and makes no sense. How many virgins, after all, does one need all at once? Whoa! Now we're getting at it. Talk about your Existential Questions!

And what of the proffered virgins themselves? Are they being rewarded or punished? Are they formerly human, permanently divine or temporarily hired? It strikes me that this is a form of concubinage. Second-class citizens in life, war booty in the afterlife. I tell you, it's a raw deal!

And what of female martyrs? Is there some sort of separate-but-equal clause for them? What is their reward? How many boys/men do they get? And are their young men virgins? Is this ever addressed??

Having grown up in a litigious society, I am aware of the importance of detail and fine print in a solid contract. If I were prone to martyrdom (which I am most decidedly not), I would want my deal sealed tight before I jumped off the edge. No vague promises for me. I've seen the bait and switch before, thank you very kindly.

Actually this whole thing strikes me as a scam. It has that slightly sleazy, skewed feel of a recruiting ploy. I don't doubt that the Marines could have reeled me in with that one straight out of high school. But the virgins would have had to be in this lifetime. Even then I understood that chasing an erection around was only something I would get to do/have to do in this lifetime. In the next, I would be much more serene and cerebral. I would exist on an ethereal, spiritual plane, eat manna, hang with angels and contemplate my own perfect self. I would certainly not be mucking about in things carnal, concerning myself with seducing women, virginal or otherwise.

No, this whole thing has a human smell to it. Specifically, it has an adult, male aroma. I do not believe that this is the Voice of God proclaiming **His/Her Word**. This is not the **Hand of the Lord** writing on the wall here. I submit that these were secular schemers trying to induce young, gullible, hormone-driven saps to do something stupid that they, the adults, wouldn't dream of doing. Virgins, my ass! They understood sexual repression and were just lining up18-year-olds to exploit for generations to come for their own benefit.

Understand that I'm not casting aspersions on abstinence or mocking in any way the virginal state here. I think abstinence is a prudent and wise thing. The older I get, the more admirable and intelligent it becomes. It certainly simplifies individual and societal order and sidesteps some very treacherous health concerns. The issue here is not sexual activity. The issue is this mythical and enforced virginal state.

Which by the way is pretty much impossible to prove or disprove. This membrane I mentioned, the hymen, is both amazingly flexible and extremely fragile. The way I read it, most are long gone before the first sexual partner. But some even survive childbirth. Its "intactness" is neither medically demonstrable nor legally provable. So the status of a woman in this regard is a matter of self-declaration. Unless someone claims "knowledge", in the Biblical sense. (Yet another euphemism.) This, in some cultures, can be a life and death matter.

There is precedent here in the Animal World. Male stallions and Alpha males of all stripes and species zealously and vigorously defend harems of breeding females. However, they don't care a whit about their sexual history. They don't have a lot tied up in being first. They are driven solely to enforce the imperative that their seed will determine the future of their species. It may sound egotistical, but it's really just Nature driven.

But this human virginity battle is not about lineage. This doesn't have anything to do with procreation or paternity. Virginity, as I see it, is not so much a condition as some idealized version of Woman– meek, submissive, protected. It is the version History is surging to overtake.

So this strikes me as one of those troublesome exclusivity issues. It is a domain thing and is intermingled with property rights and the male ego–a dangerous combination. Ultimately, of course, it's about Power. And when Power begins to ebb, there is conflict. The Insecure first become threatened, then illogical and finally dangerous. It is a sad and frightening state of affairs. But I suppose it is the way of things. I suppose it must be so when we are caught in History's wake.

Coat Conundrum

…in which Uncle Duke compares marriage and the Civil War.

I have a few thoughts on the Confederate Flag. Diana and I discuss it often. Except in our case it's about my sport coat. It's kind of a lime-green madras affair, and I've had it since college. Or maybe high school. But it hides its age well, and I admit I am pretty proud of the fact that it still fits. I like the way I look in it. In my mind it makes my shoulders broader and my hips slimmer. And it definitely has a festive flair to it, particularly in the Summer. Gin and tonic in hand, I can feel myself swaggering a little when I wear it.

Diana does not see it in the same light. She does not think it flatters me, nor does she think it flatters her when I wear it. She thinks it is a testament to youthful bad taste and middle aged obstinacy. In short, she is offended by it. She has not gone so far as to say that I embarrass her when I wear it, but then she doesn't need to.

It is a dilemma, I tell you. I feel like I have earned the right to wear whatever clothes I want to wear. Flattering or not. Stylish or not. I am the Master of what goes on my back, by God. As a male of Southern heritage, of a certain age, I have THE RIGHT to flout convention if I so choose, to tweak the noses of the elite, the *fashionistas*. If I FEEL good in it, why she and the rest of the Civilized World can suck eggs. And then get over it.

She, on the other hand, feels like we are a couple, and she is the one who, more than others (certainly more than me) has to look at me. She would like me to be pleasing to her sense of aesthetics. If we are out, and she involuntarily cringes when she looks at me, why this is not a positive experience for her. If one is in a relationship, should not one try to please the other, she asks. Do we not trade jobs, favors, responsibilities for each other's benefit? Is that not part of the deal?

She makes a good point, damn it. I surely hate it when that happens. But she is right. That is the crux of the problem. Rights vs. Responsibilities. If one wants to fly a flag (or wear a jacket) that reminds them of when they were young, teenage, broncing bucks (with a pink carnation and a pickup truck), if one wants to express their rebellious nature and their disdain for the sensitivities of others, if one wants to choose one side of the argument and wrap oneself in it to the profound displeasure of the other, well I reckon they have that Right. But if someone you need, someone who is part of your extended family, your neighborhood, or someone with whom you have a relationship is offended by it, are there not corresponding Responsibilities? Are there not Rules of Compromise that apply. Of course there are. They're in a book somewhere. Maybe even the Bible. We could look it up if we wanted.

But the real question is: Do we have a relationship? Do we want to have a relationship? Do we want to be part of the same Family? Or is it just too damn hard?

Well, given the force of Diana's argument, I have retired my sport coat. In this particular context, I do care what she thinks. And I am willing to give up an occasional Right for the prospect of pleasing her. In the light of our past and future, it is a small enough price to pay.

And it strikes me that retiring the Confederate flag is a small enough price to pay. There are many ways to honor ones' Heritage without rubbing someone else's nose in it. There may come a time when that battle flag will have a place. When wounds are healed. When pain subsides. Until then, it makes sense to lock it in our Historical trunk.

As for my coat, I have not gotten rid of it. No, sir. I know exactly where it is, and it is warm and dry. Because I fully expect bright madras fabric, maybe even lime-green sport coats, to come back into style. Any time now. And when it does, I will wrap myself in it and swagger on out. And Diana will wrap herself around me and walk proudly at my side.

A Game for All Seasons

…in which Uncle Duke reveals his love for The Game.

I confess I was not prepared for the strength of my feelings. I would never have predicted how strongly I feel about the way Caleb is coached baseball. But there it is. He's nine and playing in his first "kids pitch" league. I will say that it is tremendously thrilling to see him play, to see him move around with a uniform on. He is the center of my focus. The game revolves around him. I love to see him glide towards a ground ball or race around the bases. I would love to claim he is chipped from my block. But even as much as I am capable of shading my memory and rewriting history, I can not remember gliding across the field. What I did on the base paths was never called racing. Even I recall that persistence was by far my greatest asset as a player.

I certainly did not believe that I would be one of those dugout dads who are the bane of coaches and umpires around the country, the ones who shout ill-conceived directions and relive their youths through their children. In fairness, I don't think I am one of those. I am intensely interested, somewhat protective, excessively watchful and overwhelmingly proud. I am guilty of these parental sins, perhaps others. I should add that of these sins I am absolutely unashamed.

However, to my surprise and horror, it has become evident that I am a baseball purist. Gad, who would have thought it? I am intent on seeing baseball taught, and learned, in its purest physical and metaphysical form. Baseball as Zen exercise. Baseball as martial art. Baseball, the way I think it oughta be.

I do believe that baseball should be its own reward. The game, particularly at nine, should be a joyful experience. Fielding grounders is fun. Shagging fly balls is big fun. Hitting is ultimate fun. The joy of swinging at balls without fear of striking out, of knowing there are more pitches to come, is just about the grandest fun there is.

I think the most fun I ever had was playing baseball. Choosing up sides after school in backyards and empty lots and cow pastures. Rocks or wadded-up jackets for bases, trees or garages for foul lines, balls the color of Army jeeps. No umpires. It was the best of times.

◆ ◆ ◆

The adults, well-meaning, one and all, saw our interest and organized us into a Little League. I will say that putting on the uniform was a thrill. Playing under the lights with brand new, white balls and all that attention was a grand rush. But some of the joy and innocence left the game. It became a measure of our worth. It was their league. *They* assigned us to teams, *they* told us where to play, *they* called the balls and strikes. In short, they made all the rules. It became less a game and more an initiation into the adult world. Somehow, I never had as much fun playing baseball after I put a uniform on.

Friends who weren't very good but always played in our pick-up games ceased playing altogether when it got organized. In our games, they'd get 4, 5, even 6 strikes. The adult rules wouldn't bend like that. They never got to play much and chose not to make their lack of coordination and skill a matter of public record. In a sense, the ante went up when the adults took over. It became a game of wins and losses, of bottom lines. The results were even published in the newspaper. The victors got the spoils. The losers got toe jam.

Understand that I am not opposed to competition. There was a time when I thrived on it. The intensity required to play against someone at your own skill level or beyond is part of being fully alive. The concentration and intensity required in competitive situations allows us to stretch our abilities and see what we are capable of. Nature is full of examples of the shaping value of competition. And there is competition that goes on around the edges of every pick-up game. This is valuable stuff. I'm just not sure it's terribly valuable at 9.

◆ ◆ ◆

So, it's the first game of the year and Caleb is batting. I am anxious and fearful and hopeful, my unenlightened worst. I hear a loud, male voice yell: "Strike him out, Todd!" And I am literally stunned. It had somehow not dawned on me that the other team wanted my son to fail, that their success depended to a large degree on our failure. And they wanted that to happen. Caleb is an intense kid and doesn't understand much about failure at this point. He doesn't tolerate it terribly well. Who does? But he's a 3rd grader. He sometimes cries when he strikes out–not openly, but behind a tree, into his hands. His eyes get red from the strain of holding in the tears.

So anyway, Todd, to be a winner in his own and others' eyes, must diminish Caleb. He must vanquish him. And in so doing he must cause pain far more intense than a beaning. If the guy had said: "Stick it in his ear, Todd!", it would have been much less jarring somehow.

What we fail to understand is that this is win-win here. Who can fail? Todd in his crisp red and white uniform and new glove, standing erect and throwing hard. Caleb in his baggy blue-and-gold, blowing bubbles and waving his bat ominously. It is no more complicated than this. The end has nothing to do with the means. The odds are that neither Todd nor Caleb will make their living playing baseball. This is not about job training or career advancement. This is not even about character development. This is about elementary fun on Saturday morning. If it does not fulfill that mission statement, then it is worthless. It is counter-productive. Why do it at all?

It's supposed to be a kids' game. But adults tend to obsessively organize things. They have high expectations. Men in particular apparently have an overwhelming need to shout advice. Mostly it is empty and ill-conceived and unimaginative (In contrast to my own advice which is well-timed, sound and based on a fundamental knowledge of the game). Additionally, much of their advice is physiologically contradictory and untenable for sustained periods of time–such as one at-bat. "Cock your elbow," they yell, with voices that could shatter Plexiglas. "Choke up!" "Keep your weight back!" "Follow through!" All good advice, to be sure. But now is not the time. They shout instructions which are supposed to replace hours of practice, hundreds of internalized corrections. See, kids know how to play. If it's important to them, they figure out what they're doing wrong and make adjustments. It's not that tough a game. Pitch, catch, swing, run, slide. Do it again. A couple million repetitions and it's like you've been doing it all your life. But no amount of bonehead adult advice will make them any better.

Well, I want to yell stuff too. I want to be the voice in the back of Caleb's head, the one that sounds like his own, saying: "It's just a game. Have fun." I want to shield him from all the other nonsensical adult voices telling him where to put his hand and how to distribute his weight and all the other crap that didn't exist before they invented baseball analysts who started expounding it. I want to hit him grounders til he says, "That's enough, Dad." I want to hit him fly balls til he gets tired or bored and the smile leaves his face. I want to play catch til all our balls are in the storm sewer, or my arm hurts too much. Then we'll go buy some more. Or I'll take some Advil.

See, we're throwing back and forth more than just baseballs here. This is affection. This is respect. This is trust. It's a game where no one keeps score, no one loses and no one wears a uniform. It is Summer. The sun is out. It is the best of times.

IV

Unanswered Questions

Rites of Passage

...in which Uncle Duke examines Death and Rebirth.

This time of year, the highways are covered with evidence of our overwhelming desire to begin anew. We call it road kill. It is an unpleasant reminder of our own mortality and our own compulsion to get to the other side of the road. It can be pretty ugly–irregular shapes of fur and feathers, intestines and bones spread out on the road, former life-forms smashed and splattered on the asphalt or bounced into the drainage ditches. It makes us pretty uncomfortable, and we go to great lengths to avoid the mooshed corpses. Even in this Age, we recognize some connection between them and ourselves.

Evolution has not prepared animals well for the automobile. It came along so fast. They are ill prepared for 3000-pound metal monsters with great bright, transfixing eyes, racing at them at 60 miles per hour. Their instincts tell them to cross the road. The air is saturated with the smell of unlimited possibilities. Their hormones demand that they venture across. The sweet, glandular secretions from ready females and randy males beck-on them, promising mating opportunities, copulatory delights.

So testosterone-soaked raccoons sniff at the roadside, weigh the risks, and then, with lust in their hearts, waddle off to their deaths. And despondent possums, losers in love, rejected suitors, lumber out onto the road and throw themselves into the paths of speeding trucks. Graceful deer, assured by their athleticism and imagining Elysian Fields of clover and corn, discard caution and leap blindly into traffic. Snakes slither their cold-blooded bodies out onto the warm blacktop to soak up the heat and wind up twisted, reptilian ropes on country roads all across America. Turtles find that the path to enlightenment and self-fulfillment often crosses other more dangerous paths. They resign themselves to the perilous journey and set out. Turtles are slow. The odds are long.

Cats and dogs make bad choices and wind up under buses every day. Cats cannot resist their curiosity, and dogs blunder out for no particular reason. Rabbits, confident in their quickness, dart in front of cars and wind up a hare too slow. Squirrels, awash in indecision, flit back and forth and ultimately underneath fat, black tires. Even hawks and owls, incredulous at their good fortune, land to feast at the roadside bounty and become matted feathers themselves.

There is a prominent theory that life exists poised between order and chaos. In the same way, all of us multiply and thrive or diminish and subsist based on the delicate dance we do between foolhardy courage and excessive caution. Each evening this scene is played out millions of times along the highways of the world–to risk or not to risk. What are the chances? Is the benefit worth the risk? What are my odds? We see the losers at this game–those who gambled the family jewels and left them for ravens on the pavement, those who wagered their DNA and lost it in the headlights. This is a cruel time of year.

About this time every year, I am reminded of Lester Simpson. Lester was from my hometown. He was one of a number of diminished individuals around there we termed "retarded". In small towns, they existed at the fringes of society and were pretty much allowed to do as they pleased. Everyone knew them and watched out for them. He ate all his meals at Cecconi's Restaurant, and I never saw him pay. Billy Mayes never charged him for his haircuts either, I don't think. I would guess he was around 40 when I knew him, though I could be off by 20 years in either direction. I never knew where he lived. Or if he ever went to school. There weren't many details available. He was just Lester.

Lester could most often be found walking along the highways of Washington County. He would pick up trash and put it in bags. I believe the Rotary Club paid him 50 cents a bag. The Highway Department gave him an official reflector vest and a yellow hard hat which he wore with some pride.

Lester's main function though was as the self-appointed mourner for animals killed along the highway. Walking the county roads, he came upon them up-close and personal. He didn't drive on by like the rest of us. Their deaths affected him. He carried with him a number of shoe boxes, supplied by Cunningham's Men's Store, and a fox-hole shovel. When he came across an unfortunate animal, he would gently scoop the remains in one of those shoeboxes and bury them along the roadside. When it was laid to rest, he would conduct a small ceremony with head bowed and hands folded. He was the minister, the pall bearer, the grieving family and the congregation. He represented all of us. No one knew the contents of those prayers. Or who they were directed to. But it is true that Lester always wiped his eyes and blew his nose when he was done. They were genuine prayers all right, as sincere as there was in that county. More than most probably.

Later he would mark the spot with a crude wooden cross made out of scrap lumber they'd give him at Pettus Lumber. If there were wildflowers available, or someone's garden nearby, he would sprinkle the grave with fresh flowers. The roads in Washington County were covered with silent memorials to animals that died trying to get to the other side.

This is an intense time of year, on many levels. There are moments of terror, frozen instants of dark realization, when flight is not an option. When death is inevitable. There are moments when the Truth is overwhelming. I believe that those moments are held in place somewhere. The silent screams are recorded in time and space and become part of the permanent history of the planet.

Well, Lester understood the terror. He felt the panic. He heard the screams. It's true he may have been slower than the rest of us. And he didn't focus on the same things. But I don't know that his days weren't more meaningful or more profound. I'm not sure the things he thought about weren't more important and that he didn't do a better job of keeping the Universe in balance than any of us.

Spring is all about renewal. But the act of renewal requires closure. We must grieve for that which passes before rebirth can occur. Lester was our designated mourner. He was our witness. He laid the wild things to rest. And ushered in The Spring.

Divine Music

...in which Uncle Duke reaches for the Eternal.

I confess I do not believe in a whole lot anymore. Over time, most of what I grew up believing has proven itself rather hollow and mostly baseless. Bad myth accounted for most of it. Although it sustained my parents well enough, it has not brought me great comfort. I have spent a lifetime sorting through it all.

Things temporal were the first to go. I arbitrarily chose 100,000 years as a guidepost. My reasoning was that if it hadn't been around at least that long, it hadn't stood the test of Time. That took care of You and Me, both Houses of Congress and basically everything else We have built. In one fell swoop.

That pretty much took care of God too—the Western One anyway. Although it is argued that God has been around forever, that He/She/It in fact invented Time, I don't hear anyone claiming that God took any sort of active role in Universal affairs until Men and Women stood upright and evolved as sentient beings. Although God ostensibly created the Universe and Life as we know it, it appears He was at best a passive manager throughout the first 14 billion years or so. To hear those who seem to know about these things tell it, God was basically uninvolved until We came along, developed opposable thumbs and began grasping and inventing interesting vices. To say that this God is Human-centered is an immense understatement. Humans alone "are created in His Image and Likeness"? Come on! This strikes me as arrogant, dismissive and short-sighted. I'm sorry. I reject the Notion.

I am not without beliefs however. I do believe in Biology. It passes the 100,000 year test and has been operating by a very precise set of rules at least since cells began to divide and algae ruled the World. It is intensely organized, logical and does not play favorites. As we begin to understand the secret lives of bacteria and sperm whales, the way cells and species interact, the way the intricate details of Life play out on both micro and macro scales, the marvels of Biology are revealed. If one admires efficiency, it is both beautifully and brutally efficient. It is a system that is both unyielding and inventive. Biology works! I'm thinking about switching my major.

Lately I am increasingly drawn to those things fundamental and elementary. And nothing is more fundamental and elementary than Chemistry. It reduces everything to its most basic elements. And Chemistry predates Biology even. The rules of the chemical game are immutable and timeless. The equations simultaneously bore and confound me; but it is a marvelous system, and I am a big fan.

I also believe in Physics, Astronomy, Geology, Cosmology. All that stuff. I believe in Time so immense it is fearsome to contemplate. These subjects are all built on the premise of minuscule changes over incomprehensible Time. I might add that I don't understand Them. Hardly at all. Furthermore, I don't believe anyone alive has much more than glimpsed Their Secrets. They are silent and irrevocable and awesome, perhaps beyond our comprehension. But I believe our Origin and our Destiny are waiting in that boundless expanse, that wonderful abyss, of the Undiscovered.

More than anything though, I believe in Music. Music was there at the Beginning. Music was in fact born simultaneously with Physics. Air passed from areas of high pressure to areas of low pressure. When it passed through a restriction, Energy was emitted in wave form. Which became Sound. Which became Music. It was born of the harmonic resonance of wood and metal and of vibrating chords in tension. It was born of the kinetic energy of one solid striking another and of the rhythm of ocean waves.

When the Animal world came along, they took Music from Physics to Art. They took it out of the world of random and into the world of subtlety and significance. They developed It the way horn players develop their craft. They gave It Shape–lyricism, tension and crescendo. They filled the media of air and water with transcendent Music. They created an Aesthetic of style and grace that was at once Form and Function. And We developed into that World.

Early Man understood the importance of Music. Prehistoric flutes, made up to 57,000 years ago, indicate the importance of Music to our Ancestors. The Musical instruments were more complex than the hunting tools. There was a reason for that infusion of energy into something that did not put meat on our bones or protect us from the elements. The Music was at our core then, and It remains so now.

The first thing we know is the baseline beat of our Mother's rhythmic heart, thumping away inches from our little aqueous homes. It is that profundo beat onto which we build melodies and harmonies and symphonies.

Music is the gateway to the soul. It is the passage to the heart. It fills voids we didn't know we had and leads us to greater things. There are those famous endorphins which flood our brains when we hear treasured Music. There is Music which makes us cry. Sometimes for no apparent reason. A chord touches remembrance and we are instantly linked to things past and profound.

Music hath charms, it is true, to touch angry souls. It can quiet the background noise and allow the calm to come and reside, even in the most tormented souls, if only for a time.

I believe in Music as Magic, as a medium which elevates and transforms and motivates without strings or wires or mirrors. It's in the Ether and leaps across Time and Space, fires up crusty synapses and sets them free. We will be eternally linked to the Music that was playing when we were developing independent brains and unique ideas, when our glandular buckets were sloshing over and we left teenage juices on everything we touched. We hear that Music and we are transported to that time.

The Music resonates in ancestral caves and touches ancient roots. I find I am moved beyond reason by ancient Celtic rhythms. And the gentle voices of Gregorian Chant make my Spirit soar. I conclude I have been pre-tuned by my heritage to vibrate with Anglo-Saxon and Roman Catholic frequencies. It is literally in my Bones. Those somber beats and sweet dulcimer notes put me in a place of some mystery and clarity. I hear a bagpipe and I get chills. Long fiddle riffs heat my Kentucky blood and make my feet want to tap and dance. Bluegrass banjos pluck my hard, old heart strings and make me ache. It resonates and reaches some deep place where I seldom go. The Music finds a timeless place and helps to balance me in the here and now. Which is what Religion does for some. For me, it is the Music.

It became clear to me recently that it is for others as well. Darryl and Laura have been friends of mine since high school. I was in their wedding. Their only child is 29 now. He stares blankly at the wall. At this age, he has lived longer than the doctors said he would. But his empty eyes are joyless and his body is tense. He can not speak, and he had not ever smiled.

Until three years ago. Someone put on The Planets by Gustav Holst, and his eyes flickered somewhat. As the piece progressed, his hands began to relax. Then his legs, and finally his shoulders. And as the momentum built, a genuine, clear smile grew on his face. At the end, when the heavenly chorus came in, a small tear appeared in the corner of his eye. He was in the Presence of the Divine. He was listening to the Voice of God.

Darryl and Laura had discovered the Key. For him, The Planets is a place of joy and liberation. It is an unexplained connection to emotion and feeling that we didn't know existed. And it works every time. The Power of the Music overwhelms him. For him, it is a place celestial and full. For him, it is Truth and Light. It is the Universe speaking. For him, it is the Music that's Divine.

Food for Thought

...in which Uncle Duke reveals his taste, or lack thereof.

My theories on food are not widely held. Strictly on the basis of good health, good taste and common sense, I admit that that's probably a good thing. But in terms of personal energy conservation, raw-boned economics and extending the life of our landfills, I hold that my way deserves consideration.

Actually, I cannot claim to have formulated entirely my own philosophies about food. They came directly down from my mother and, one presumes, her mother and her mother's mother. They hold basically that time spent in the kitchen preparing food is time poorly spent. Cooking for her was not an avenue of artistic expression but rather a form of homemaking drudgery, not unlike lugging dirty clothes down to the river and beating them with rocks. She waited impatiently for years for the scientific community to invent a pill that would satisfy completely our daily nutritional requirements and eliminate unnecessarily cluttering her kitchen.

My father was not overly demanding at the table. Having survived a Depression and a couple of World Wars, food on the table was not something that one had the right to grumble about. His only real requirements were in terms of color. A good meal consisted of something brown, something green and something white or yellow. Any substitutions were extremely suspect. One assumes that little pills would have been OK with him as long as they came in the proper colors. But the lines between them needed to be well defined. He was a man who respected boundaries; and if corn was meant to be mixed in with peas, why the good Lord would have put them on the same stalk.

So my culinary eccentricities have ancestral, bedrock roots. I was unprepared for a world where food, literature, art and philosophy have equal weight. In my world, soup and vegetables come from a can. Meat comes from cows and pigs and is cooked in a skillet. Exotic foods are parts of the chicken normally thrown away and aquatic life historically used for bait. One can exist on eggs and potatoes for indefinite periods of time. Peanut butter and jelly are two courses of a very nutritious and satisfying meal.

Spice racks are things you get from people you barely know when you get married and are entirely ornamental except when you make cinnamon toast. That is mostly what I know about food and, more or less, all I care to know.

Except for leftovers–or as I prefer to call them, previously prepared foods. Leftovers are the building blocks of the Universe. Never mind what those physicists say. With leftovers, I am a chef of extraordinary flair and sense of daring. Flexibility and ingenuity are the keys. There is something about working with foodstuffs that are on the outer edges of their viability. There is a profound challenge in salvaging those Tupperware wonders, those Mason jar mysteries, those bits and pieces of culinary remainders and making them into what you could call a meal. The techno-gods invented microwaves and made them cheap enough for me to afford for just this purpose.

My theory is that Americans as a whole give up on their leftovers too soon. They are, by and large, overly squeamish. I am as sensitive to inordinate color changes in food as the next guy. But I feel there is a certain amount of bacteria that is good for the body. Mold has its benefits too, you know. I consider it a form of self-immunization against food poisoning, botulism and the like to consume moderate quantities of food just slightly over the hill. I've been to Mexico a number of times and to I-don't-know-how-many company picnics, and I hardly ever get sick. I rest my case.

But I hesitate to make these views known in today's world. The passionate epicures, the food-as-art crowd, are a surly bunch and tend to look down on us food-as-sustenance, if-it-tastes-good-eat-it types. My sister-in-law refuses to eat a hard-boiled egg if she thinks I've had a hand in its preparation.

Well, I can't say that I normally mind how I'm perceived. But in this instance, at this time of year, I tend to soft-pedal my hardline foodisms. I don't want to miss out on a single potluck supper invitation. I may not know food, but I know what I like.

Mr. Haydon's Father

...in which Uncle Duke reveals a story of Darkness and Light.

I don't often think of my Grandpa Haydon. He died before I was born. But I did last night. I woke up in the middle of the night and there he was– the living image of him, or at least of that black and white photo of him that hung over the mantle. The one with his fedora on, stern-looking, about my age now. And I spoke to him from some place I didn't quite recognize. "Thank you," I said, to the man I'd never met. "Thank you for being a friend to my Father. He told me once that you were the best friend he ever had. He told me he missed you terribly after you died. And for all his years thereafter."

He stared at his shoes for awhile. He cleared his throat. "I liked Joe a lot," he said. "I liked him and respected him."

I was deeply touched by our conversation. So much so that I got up and wrote it down so it wouldn't be lost in that middle-of-the-night fog of half-remembering and forgetting. I was touched because this was not a simple relationship. Even as fathers and sons go. It was a relationship between a patriarch and his heir designate. This was a relationship also between an employer and an employee– men who later became business partners. They were mentor and protégé.

It was a relationship between a father and a son whose lives would unalterably change that day in 1910 when the son, who was then 7, shot and killed his father's fair-haired, 5-year-old daughter.

◆ ◆ ◆

I actually know very little about Grandpa Haydon. I know he had very little respect for his own father, though I don't know why. I know he farmed for awhile. I know he married a rich man's daughter and raised his family in the fine Victorian house on Main Street that his father-in-law had built. I know he helped bring electricity to our little town and allowed his oldest daughter to marry an Irishman, when many in that town wouldn't. I know he became a successful business man in his own right, and eventually bought and operated what became Haydon Mill and Grain as well as a couple of farms. But that's about it. Only two generations removed, and I know so little.

In another Age, I would know all the stories of my grandparents. In another Culture, I would know their stories as well as the stories of their grandparents, and their grandparents' grandparents. On back through Ancient Mists. And my children would know those stories as well as their own. It would have been my responsibility to make sure that they knew. But this Age does not encourage that. This Culture does not foster that. So this is a short story. It is a story without much background. Because I know so little. But it is a rich story, about a Father and a Son, full of forgiveness and redemption. It is about a Son who, even more than most, needed his Father's friendship. And a Father wise enough to understand that and compassionate enough to give it.

◆ ◆ ◆

After they buried that little girl–Martha was her name–they hardly spoke of her. They could not grieve in the usual way. The accident had made that impossible. They had the living to try and protect and allow to heal. They put her in the ground and pretended that she had never really been. They gave all their attention to the survivors. One assumes they decided they would try to deflect the shame and the guilt by the force of their love. They would protect and defend. They would march on without looking back.

It was an imperfect solution of course. Both the Present and the Future demand all of the Past. You cannot pick and choose. They were a wounded family, and Joe Haydon was a wounded man.

But I honor their intention. I honor the strength of their conviction and their capacity to bear pain, to do what they deemed necessary. I honor their resolve. In particular, I honor Grandpa Haydon who, by all accounts, stood by his son, taught him his work ethic, paid for an education well beyond the norm of the time, encouraged him and mentored him. He gave his time freely and offered his son a most cherished friendship.

◆ ◆ ◆

"Before you go," I said, "that was your pistol, wasn't it?" He stared at me without replying. "And you left it loaded, in a place where a 7 year-old could find it." No response. "There was more than my father's guilt in that house, wasn't there?" He looked away, and his silence was heart-wrenching.

"I forgive you," I said. "We all do. Just as you forgave your son. Things happen. It's what you do afterwards that matters. Thank you." He nodded, tipped his hat and faded away.

◆ ◆ ◆

It was a powerful dream. I'm honored that he came. I'm glad I had the opportunity to meet him. And I'm glad I had the chance to thank him. It's a fine story, and I'm glad I got up and wrote it down. But I don't think I would have necessarily shared it. There are many powerful stories in my family. In all families really. And there are many more unfolding every day. We can't share them all, can we?

But this morning, when I looked at the back of the framed picture, the one of him and Grandma Haydon, the one that my sister had given me, the Christmas before. And when I saw his birthday was April 16th...and when I realized that today was April 16th, somehow the story got more powerful. Somehow it became more than an imaginary encounter between me and my long-deceased Grandfather. It became a kind of spiritual connection. It became less a dream and more a real-time visitation. It became a tactile, inter-generational, hands-reaching-across-Time encounter. "Why, darn by the Devil!" I have heard he would say. My sentiments exactly, Sir. Couldn't have said it better.

So I pass it on. I introduce you to Grandpa Haydon– George Lloyd Haydon Sr.–4/16/1860-11/10/1943. I thank him for those few things I know about and the many I don't. I thank him for his hard work and perse-verance, and his wisdom and compassion through difficult times. And I pass along my sincere birthday wishes.

Humility in My Drawers

...in which Uncle Duke details the complexity of putting on your pants.

Is it just me or is everything more complicated? Take underwear for instance. Now I have been putting on my own underwear for most of my life. There were a few days I missed in there, but it's been pretty much something I've done at least once a day for some time now. You would think I'd have it down. But here's the deal. The tag used to always be on the inside and on the back. It was consistent, predictable. I like that in underwear. Now, sometimes the tag is on the outside. And sometimes it's on the front. Or even the side. This is confusing. I now know for a fact that there are exactly four different ways you can put on your underwear. I have counted them more than once. Three of them are wrong. Which is a lot. And actually you can get it wrong more times than that if you repeat some of your mistakes more than once. I have done as many as five iterations on some occasions. And once did six. Trust me when I say this. Thinking about it, which one does considerable of after about the third try, is counterproductive. Some days, it's just better to go without.

The other thing is that even when you get them oriented right, there's still the matter of hitting the leg hole dead center. I don't recall this being as much of a problem previously. But that hole seems to be getting further and further away. That's a long way down there. Of course it's dark when I get up. And my hand-eye coordination isn't so good before I've had my coffee. But there you are, buck naked, about as vulnerable as a body can get. I tell you, some days it's like jumping off a cliff.

You know the drill. One must put all one's weight on one foot. This seems to be, more and more lately, a dicey proposition. Then you lift the off leg, and in one deft motion, you simultaneously jerk the boxers/briefs/panties upwards and spear them with your pointy foot. From an engineering perspective, there's really a lot going on here. And it has to be a clean hit. If you miss entirely or, worse, snag the edge, there are likely to be some center-of-gravity issues that follow. Then you've got to do it all over again, on the other side. This doubles the odds for a bad outcome.

To make matters worse, if one is holding on to one's underwear with two hands, that leaves exactly no hands to be used for balance and/or breaking the fall. I have not yet been to the ER, but I probably should have gone that one time. Who knew there were so many pointy edges and sharp corners in a bedroom? Ouch! No sir, you can't tell me things aren't harder. Personally, I think the time is ripe for some kind of underwear holder, a combination walker/shoehorn contraption that evens the odds a bit in an old guy's favor. Maybe the AARP can sponsor a competition. Sooner the better, I say.

Autumn Passion

...in which Uncle Duke peeks into his parents' bedroom.

There was a moment (embarrassingly not that long ago) when I realized that my parents may have, at some point in their lives, had sex. They had four children, so at least more than twice would be my guess.

I remember it came as somewhat of a shock. I did not think of them, as a general rule, in *that way*. To imagine my parents in, you know, intimate terms, was perplexing, even disturbing. They were, in my recollection, disciplined, rational, organized–supremely dispassionate and decidedly unphysical. Come on! They were **Adults**, for Christ's sake!

My perception is that this is fairly standard thinking. It gives most of us the serious willies to think of our parents in the throes of passion. This is way more information than we know what to do with. *"E-e-e-e-u-w!"* we recoil. "Not *my parents*!" It's like we're talking about a couple of warthogs in rut. Snails paired in slimy rapture. Yu-u-ck! Adult sex is somehow a little creepy when we are talking about adults much older than ourselves. We are certainly ill-equipped to deal with parents in passion.

Having at some point, fairly recently actually, become an Adult myself, I am drawn to examine this. And I find that it is no wonder it is so awkward. Mostly, we are not very comfortable with THE SUBJECT of sex. We are not good at explaining the Facts of Life. Oh, we'll take a swipe at the Biology of it from time to time, but as a rule we get pretty darn squeamish around the actual Nuts and Bolts of it. We bale on the Meat and Potatoes end of it.

And even when it comes to our own grown-up sexuality, we run and hide like outlaws. We conceal it from our children like some kind of bathroom function. We isolate ourselves, close the doors and batten the hatches. It is usually a pretty involved, secretive drill. With lots of planning. "Activate sound barriers! Barricade perimeters! Woop, woop! We're going in!"

Kids have historically benefited from this actually. Many children's summer camp experiences can be attributed to their parents' desire to regain, if only for a time, a normal, spontaneous sex life. Those camps know

107

this, by the way. That's why they can charge such high rates. The price for a little liberated sex is pretty inflated these days.

It hasn't always been this way. When families lived in two or three rooms and moms and dads were putting out strings of babies year after year, physical unions were obviously quite common and not at all concealable. All that procreating wasn't going unnoticed. There's a limit to how quiet you can be. And somebody was always awake, you bet.

I've never quite gotten it. I don't know why we hide. As a culture, I'm not sure who we're trying to protect. And from what. Do we want our kids to believe that they were immaculately conceived? It may be that we are so uncomfortable around the issue of sex that we act like it doesn't happen. If we were "caught", we'd have to explain it, talk about it, personalize it in some way– just the things, it seems to me, this culture needs to de-juvenilize sex, to make it more meaningful and less superficial. But what do I know?

Someone told me recently that the greatest gift we can give our children is a happy marriage. And you've got to admit that the aforementioned is a component of that. Now in this culture, we go to great lengths to laud the three elements of partnership in our marriages. There is a) Cooperation. There is b) Trust. And there is c) Affection. These we proudly display. Then there is d) The Consummate Physical Act–the one that combines the First Three, the one that began the whole miraculous transformation of proteins into Life in the first place. The one that set us on the Path. The Crown Jewel of Married Life, for Christ's sake. This one we hide, muffle and disaffirm.

I broached this subject once. With my mother in her 80's, I asked about her and my father's sex life. I fully expected her to blush and fumble for words. Instead, her chin rose perceptibly, and her shoulders squared. "We had a long and wonderful love life," she said. Her voice was strong and without a tinge of embarrassment. "Your father was a very thoughtful and sensitive lover." Her head high, the corners of her eyes grinned at the thought. "We used to laugh that we were active long after most of our friends." How she knew that I don't know, but it amused her still. I must say she looked pretty darned smug about it. And the smile lingered in her eyes.

I was pleased to hear about my father too. I have plenty of images of him in my memory bank as President of the Rotary Club, Commissioner of the Water District, Chairman of Farm-City Week–you know, responsible, adult roles. But I have none of him with a leer in his eye. I must say it gives me great pleasure to think of him as a randy old goat. It rounds out his image and makes him much more approachable in our little imaginary, after-life conversations. It opens up our range of topics, that's for sure.

I don't know. Maybe it's because my parents are both gone. Maybe because I'm older. But I find the thought of them involved in physical love very endearing. I actually like to think of them together now. I imagine them with the house empty, the coast clear, after we were all gone. Retired and without time constraints, taking naps, cuddling up. Later in life, the old bed creaking away...

It warms my heart. It really does. It gives them another dimension, more depth somehow. In my mind, I close the door quietly and walk on down the hall.

A Fermenting Question

...in which Uncle Duke examines his own checkered past and his son's future.

My son Caleb is 14. He's got hair in places he didn't used to, and his voice is deeper than mine. It is time for a wise and mature Father to explain the mysteries and treacheries of alcohol. But as in most other areas I have had to try to explain lately, I am not qualified. Or perhaps I am overqualified. In any case, I am still much too embroiled in the mysteries and treacheries myself to clearly lay them out for him. He needs a good male role model here–but unfortunately, I'm going to have to do.

Probably I should start at the beginning–at my very first episode of teenage chugging and liberated silliness. We were 17, and it of course led to marathon hurling as our adolescent bodies tried to reject the poisons we'd gleefully consumed. I remember waking up the next morning, amidst the carnage of the previous evening, with that dreadful throbbing headache, library paste for saliva, surrounded by that ghastly, sour smell of human puke. I looked around foggily, and I remember thinking: *"That was FUN!"* The benefits outweighed the costs. There it was. The liberation was greater than the penalties. And alcohol has been a part of my life, to some degree, ever since.

The culture certainly rewards it. Even without the advertising, which is massive and sustained and brilliant, we are still a society which exalts and applauds alcohol use. In particular, there is a cultural bias that says that drinking is a manly sport. For generations males have passed through the portals into adulthood drunk on our butts. It is the way it has always been done. Drinking and sex were the adult indicators, and mostly we combined them. Generally this diminished both exercises, but never mind.

It is said that Eskimo people have dozens of words for the snow which plays such a prominent and essential role in their lives. We have hundreds of words for being drunk. Blasted, wasted, shnockered, bombed, hammered, sloshed, ripped, blotto, crushed, potted, smashed...I could go on. So could you.

You will notice that most of these conditions are not ones into which we would normally put ourselves, voluntarily at least. But we do. We happily hit ourselves over the head with very big, blunt alcohol hammers without a great deal of embarrassment or self-reflection. We drink with passion, intensity, consistency, and not a little pride.

It is hard to explain to a 14 year old why we do that. What is the appeal of a beer after work? A drink before dinner? I don't really have a good answer. I guess the key word though is liberation. In our work-a-day world, one must hold so tightly to reality. And the voices of reality are not always forgiving. A friend once told me: "I'd do anything to get out of my own head," as he popped another cold one. We are, many of us anyway, uncomfortable in our own heads. Our own voices are often disparaging. They are the voices of critical parents, demanding teachers or just our own perfectionist yearnings. It is my experience that alcohol mutes those voices. Under that influence, conversations with ourselves become less argumentative, less accusatory, and more amicable. In some cases, with the correct chemical mix, the voices become even complimentary. "You are one witty son-of-a-gun, Guy. You should have your own TV show. What a card!" Flattery just rolls off our tongues.

In addition, our normal reality includes schedules and lists, places to be, people to see. Alcohol induces us into a world of the here and now. More future-based responsibilities can be postponed. We can temporarily move into the world of living in the moment that those self-help gurus all espouse. Many of us just have a hard time getting there without anaesthetizing certain critical parts of our brains.

We are by Nature social beings. But most of us creak along as shy and introverted vertebrates. Our interactions are stiff, rigid and awkward. But when we introduce alcohol into the interaction, our social joints get limber. We become participants in active human discourse. It can be a grand and liberating influence.

Weddings without bars, for example, are rather staid and formal affairs. No one dances much. And if they do, you don't see much real booty-shaking. Jesus himself chose just such an occasion to perform His first miracle. When the wine ran out, He made more. And although the accounts don't actually mention it, my assumption is that as the celebrants got lubricated in the second half of the reception, they became less self-conscious and very inventive. "Hoo-wee! I'm smoking now," those Canaanites said, as they bumped, jerked, boogied, bunny-hopped and hokie-pokied around the room. Alcohol has always unleashed the hootchie-cootchie in us. It's the nature of the Beast.

At least in the early male years, in and around high school and college, alcohol had a lot to do with women. Speaking for myself, girls were mysterious, frightening and very desirable. And I mostly felt dull and awkward around them. Those guys who attracted girls were glib, suave and smooth. My manner was wooden, clunky and overly polite. I found that alcohol unlocked what I perceived as Natural Charm. I was capable of small talk, large talk, boldness and daring. It may have been shallow success, but (Forgive me, Goddess.) shallow success was mostly what I was after. My feeling is that social awkwardness is the reason many of us began our alcohol careers. I cannot speak to the female side of the equation, but it would not surprise me if there were parallels. We all want to be cool and well liked. And it is easier to be those things, or at least feel like we are those things, when we have a snoot full.

But there is an obvious and unavoidable Dark Side. There is a lot of pain out there. There are many for whom the excessive clarity of sobriety is overwhelming. For them, life is only bearable when they are sedated. Alcohol is a cheap and accessible over-the-counter medication. The only question is frequency and dosage. How much does it take, and how often?

This culture talks a lot about Drugs. And it is absolutely true that there are thousands and thousands of lives lost to illegal, addictive drugs every year. And the health care costs associated with tobacco are staggering. No argument. My assumption though is that those figures pale in comparison to alcohol's. The prisons and emergency rooms and therapists' offices in this country are stacked with the effects of alcohol. But the public service announcements consist of refrains to let someone else drive you home when you get shit-faced. There are no TV spots that say: "This is your brain on tequila," with worms crawling through a mess of scrambled eggs. We pretty much soft-pedal the harmful effects of alcohol in deference to selling the product with slick humor and big hooters. There's too much money on the table. If you want the truth about alcohol, you've got to dig it up yourself.

So, back to Caleb. What do I tell him? Do I want him to drink? Or does it matter? Have I already shown him what I think by how and when I drink? I am not proud of all aspects of my relationship with alcohol over the years, but I have told him as much. And I have tried to be specific about the parts I thought were healthy and those that were less so. My hope is that my usage has been measured enough to model. My hope is that moderation counts. And that my honesty will be worth something.

Supply and Demand

...in which Uncle Duke looks at the economies of vices.

I am not an economist. Have no interest in the subject. But the economics of our vices are certainly a curiosity to me. I've heard that Capitalism is the cornerstone of this country. It is, I understand, the philosophical center over which the Cold War was fought. The mantra of the Market–"Give the people what they want"–apparently brought down the Berlin wall and the Communist System which held it upright all those years. America has tirelessly promoted Capitalism and the Free Market System since its inception. This is all well and good.

Now, however, we have intentions of decertifying our nearest trading partner for not doing enough to shut down the supply of drugs. As I see it, we are going to penalize Mexico for responding to market demands. Let me get this straight. The United States is the biggest consumer of drugs in the world. We smoke, snort and inject everything the Third World produces and pay top dollar for it. We essentially drive the market. And now we point our fingers at an economically struggling country for adopting the Capitalist Manifesto and responding to the rich market that we create. That takes a lot of gall, it seems to me.

The Pharmaceutical Industry is able to profit enormously from the sale of drugs which make people feel better. Americans pay drug companies vast sums each year for substances which rearrange our brain molecules, reconstitute our chemicals and activate our pheromones to give us a sense of well-being. They quiet the little voices, give us some internal peace and keep us from acting out. Doctors can't get out their prescription pads fast enough. In the medical/psychiatric field, drugs are largely the answer. There are no age restrictions, by the way. If you can pay (or your parents can), you can get sedated. Do we hear Just Say No to Prozac? Get serious! How about Ritalin-free Zones around our schools? Not on your life! The difference is somewhat blurred to me.

Alcohol companies provide us with a vast array of products which, let's not kid ourselves, scramble our brain cells and muddy the water sufficiently so we can feel competent, confident and somewhat joyful for a time. They advertise heavily that their products will provide us with more fun per ounce, more contentment per bottle, more friends per tankful. They don't mention altered consciousness, but that's what it's really all about. There are vastly more human lives damaged, ruined every year by alcohol than by drugs. Infant mortality, suicide, family violence, wasted lives, property damage–the statistics are overwhelming. Yet we spend about a gazillion dollars a year advertising and promoting the use of alcohol at the same time that we pretend to try to discourage the use of drugs. I can see that. And I'm not that smart.

We experimented with making alcohol illegal, you may remember. It was, it turns out, a horrible mistake which allowed some poor men to get rich and a lot more to get dead. Our prisons got overfull. The law enforcement agencies and the legal profession profited enormously, but we expended huge amounts of energy and capital trying to stop people from doing what they wanted to do and in some cases needed to do.

It didn't work. The reason is simple. Supply and Demand. The demand was too great. When the supply diminished, people killed each other with some enthusiasm and went to jail in great numbers to try and feed it. Negative consequences, it turns out, do not extinguish the profit motive. The desperate are always willing to take the risk.

We still put people in jail for running numbers and other illegal gaming operations. Not often though. We used to do it a lot. But now that there are more gambling casinos than convenience stores, it's hard for Sam the Bookie to make a decent living. The profiteers made it legal and took over the territory. Did the morality of gambling change? Not at my church. Is it more ethical now to roll dice and play slots than it was when they were rousting out and busting up gaming houses? Not in my pew. Somehow it just got legal. Which is not the same thing at all as moral or ethical or good for the community. It just changes the way Federal prosecutors look at it.

It doesn't matter if it's good for us or not. Economics is like evolution in that sense. It doesn't know if it's good or evil. Doesn't care. That's not the issue. Alcohol, tobacco and firearms are arguably not good for us. Yet large numbers of us apparently need them in some profound way. We sell products to the needy–those people who need to assuage their pain or their fear or their anxiety or their emptiness. We buy to fill up the hole.

The same is true with the drug trade. It's a fairly simple equation really. It holds for gold, silver, plutonium–any rare element. It holds for adoptable babies, transplantable organs and Cuban cigars. If more people want it than have it, it holds. It would hold for jelly beans and Rogaine if they took them off the market. The market would demand them, a vast illegal black market would spring up to provide them for exorbitant sums, and then gangs, families and cartels would begin killing each other with malice and forethought for the territories. This isn't rocket science. This is basic economic theory with a little history thrown in. Supply and Demand. High Demand + Inadequate Supply = OPPORTUNITY. America rewards people who respond to opportunities. We call them entrepreneurs. They purchase dealerships. They offer franchises. They sell shares. A marketable product at whatever the market will bear. On the street we call them dealers. But make no mistake, they are salesmen. Bona fide businessmen. They have learned well the lessons America taught.

It is a stone-cold fact that when cartels get busted up, when drug kingpins get taken down, there is a slight, momentary dip in the supply. But other opportunists, venture capitalists of the first order, fill the gap and reopen the pipeline. The Republicans are right. The Market works.

That our sons and daughters use drugs is not the fault of the dealer. Without the pain, there would be no need. Without the need, there would be no demand. Without the demand, there would be no supply.

Mexico asks why we can't diminish the demand. Good question, Mexico.

Sons of the Fathers

...in which Uncle Duke constructs a Legacy.

I try to give my children 100 percent of my time and attention. I find however that I am about 10 minutes short every day. Which is about right. Offsprings by their nature demand about 1 percent more than they could possibly have from us. It is their job actually. I am reminded of baby birds in the nest, their mouths gaping and stretching, their necks reaching, their parents frantically flying about, stuffing worms, caterpillars, moths, frogs, French fries, small mammals, anything, into the cavernous yaws. And the mouths never close. They continually gape except to sleep. And they never sleep at the same time. Baby goats, kids actually, aggravate their mothers to death trying to get to a nipple. They are genetically programmed to want as much as they can get and then a little bit more. It is a system that has evolved over millions of years. It is a system that works.

Our children, in this day and age, in this part of the world, are for the most part well fed. They do not lack for macaroni and cheese or corn flakes. But their personalities are gaping, stretching, demanding. They require all that we have. It is their job. Our attention is the fuel that forms their personalities and their minds. Our attention is that which proves to them that they exist. And they will get it. It is a game of escalation in which the only question is when and at what cost.

There is no great mystery here. Every few years, researchers proclaim that children from families where they are talked to, listened to, read to, have better test scores and are less inclined to require shock therapy. Duhh! It is virtually impossible to spoil children with *real* attention.

On the other hand, it is very likely we will spoil them with goods in response to guilt from insufficient time and attention. We do want them to like us, and we will spend a lot of money to that end. But it's a rat hole. Our children know that money is cheap, so it's a temporary fix at best.

Besides, it is not our job to fill their toy chests. Nor is it our job to toughen them up for the difficult journey through life. It is our job to rein-force them with attention, to bolster their confidence with praise, to satu-rate them with love. If they believe they are the center of the universe, they will take up a very small portion of it. The more they are unsure, the larger and louder and more troublesome they become.

To put it mildly, I am puzzled by a lot of parenting I see. Parents do not seem to derive much joy from their children. There are parents with children on the playgrounds, putting in the time, but there are few smiles on the supervisory faces. With few exceptions, this is begrudged attention. This is not interactive play. These are the faces of prison guards, hard and resentful. These are faces that want to be somewhere else.

There appears to be a sharp, rather harsh line drawn between children and ADULTS. Children play and laugh and interact, while ADULTS supervise, bark commands and warn their charges that they will fall on their keisters and require emergency treatment. I see few parents or guardians on the monkey bars. Apparently, one must go to a fitness center and pay lots of money to do that sort of thing. Play is something adults do in casinos, not on playgrounds. I guess I don't understand.

And I suppose I am disappointed in America as well. People here seem to have the absurd notion that they can simultaneously have children and lives. I am taken aback by this. Early on, in the 80's, I was led to believe that this was so. The phrase "quality time" was being bandied about then. It was bogus, of course, another vacuous concept from that period. But there are those apparently who still believe it. The concept of children as accessories is more prevalent than we admit. Children are one component of a rich and full life, the theory goes, along with home, career, portfolio, sport utility vehicles, 150 channels and a good back swing–not necessarily in that order.

It is an unrealistic expectation. Somehow we have been led to believe, figuratively at least, that children are capable of raising themselves. We believe them to be self-nurturing. It is assumed that children, like water, will find their own levels. And it is true that they are amazingly resilient. It is true that we can raise them with partial attention and that they can get good grades, get into college, learn a trade and avoid significant jail time. As long as the terrain is smooth, they can maneuver tolerably well. But I don't believe we can ground them with partial attention. I'm not sure that we can set their internal compasses without total attention.

I really tire of rote comments from parents about their kids, the ones where they refer to them as the 11th plague, the hard payback for their sins in college, a royal pain in the posterior to be endured until they can be foisted off on some poor guidance counselor or, worse, an unfortunate spouse.

I suppose there is some therapeutic value in humor. And it is true that it always gets a good laugh. But it mostly strikes me as shallow and repetitive and tiresome. It glosses over the underlying wonder and mystery of children, the biological complexity of offsprings. That something that begins with a momentary, random physical act becomes a walking, talking individual at least as independent and disagreeable as we are is astounding to me. I confess I am in awe of the process.

I continually hear that "they'll be gone before you know it". I know this is true. I see them growing and maturing before my eyes every day. And my own mortality is no longer in doubt. I shall be gone just as my parents are. So this is serious, imminent business here. This is the most important thing that I do. I am raising myself in a sense. I am nurturing another link in the chain, the way my grandparents nurtured my parents, the way they were nurtured by their parents, and so on, back through ancient mists. To what end I am not sure. It's not for me to know.

All I do know is that I am not just raising sons here. I am raising my own descendants. And I am raising my own vision of the future. Realistically, it is the only way I have to change the world.

It's Only a Game

...in which Uncle Duke examines a lifelong obsession.

I suppose sooner or later I've got to get a handle on this Winning and Losing thing. It's an issue that won't go away on its own. I thought as I matured, it would take care of itself. But it hasn't happened. Winning still feels *so* good, and losing still hurts *real* bad.

As a kid I lived and died with the University of Kentucky basketball team. The sound of legendary announcer Caywood Ledford's voice over the radio and the UK fight song filled my winter nights. Fortunately, they won with some amazing regularity. But when they lost, I would anguish and wail and break things. When they lost to Texas Western in the NCAA finals in 1966, I died numerous deaths. It was close to the end of the world.

But that was OK. Back then it was supposed to hurt. Devotion to winning was a certifiable virtue and earned high praise. Vince Lombardi and many others were still extolling winning as "the only thing", the Holy Grail, that which made life worth living. Losing was ignominy. Losing was death. Every coach I ever had subscribed to that philosophy and took a turn burning it into me.

I try now to put this in the context of latter-day 12-year-old baseball and 7-year-old soccer. It is a complicated equation and a delicate dance for a Dad. My job, as I understand it, is to harness my own inclinations and to teach the important elements of both winning and losing. And frankly, I'm not sure I'm doing such a hot job.

In most circles it is not politically correct to put much emphasis on winning at this level. There is some uneven application of this, but the leagues are still touted at least as "developmental and recreational". I mostly agree with this philosophy, but I struggle mightily with its implementation. And unless I'm mistaken, I'm not alone.

You'll notice by the way that they still keep score. And the people who are more serious about it generally win. Those people tend to celebrate more and generally have more fun on the way home. Additionally, when people who weren't there ask how you did, they don't want some vague, New Age explanation of character and cooperation and potential. They want to know this–W or L, where **W=Attaboy** and **L=Sorry, Charlie. You lose. Better luck next time.**

For better or worse, both my sons seem to have emerged from the womb with a certain bottom-line intensity. They keep score on everything. Checkers at age 4 was a Titan struggle, and whiffle ball even now will probably end in tears and accusations. I'm still picking up Monopoly hotels from that game last summer. In my defense I will say I've always tried to emphasize the fun part of games. Winning was never the object in any of the games that I made up. But it never took. They never bought it.

By the way, winning and losing used to be a male-only domain. Women clucked and chuckled at the male obsession. They cheered on the sidelines and tolerated the boys' passion for silly games. They did not share the passion. Now with their wholesale entry into the active realm of sports, that has dramatically changed. Girls and their mothers pursue the drug of winning as vehemently as boys and their fathers. They burn on the fields and on the sidelines. I'm not sure if this is a case of women catching a man's disease or competition igniting a human fire across genders. And I don't here judge it good or bad. But there it for certain is.

There do seem to be some genetic roots to the passion. Some otherwise well-adjusted individuals seem born with the passion to excel and ultimately to win. Their focus is clear. Their drive is never deterred. Whether it's chess or tennis or debate, they will persist.

Winning is after all what we are programmed to do. For generations untold, we have pursued victory as if our very lives depended on it–which of course they have. It is necessarily a primal urge to escape predators, to get the last scrap of meat, the best nesting site, the best mate. Losing to our ancestors meant subjugation and death. Second place meant someone else got to reproduce. If physical abilities were equal, it was often determination and guile and persistence which determined the Alpha male, the dominant female. That legacy is ours. If you ask me, it plays out in hockey rinks and soccer fields all over the planet. The victor still gets the spoils. This is not a well-kept secret. Only now the spoils are respect and recognition.

But while there is still a struggle going on in Little League soccer and Peewee hockey over the importance of winning, there is no such struggle going on in college and professional sports. Moral victories are not goals at this level. These teams are defined by their records. They carry the pride and self-respect of entire geographical and ideological areas on their backs.

Fans wear the colors. They shave their heads, take off their shirts in sub-zero weather and paint their bodies in team colors. We smirk at aboriginal people in National Geographic who do the same thing, without the benefit of alcohol. They gladly pay– corporately, governmentally and individually–for the privilege of Identity, particularly when the team is winning.

This is the pure and unadulterated pursuit of the DRUG of winning. For periods of time, we sublimate our difficult, uphill lives to a single, condensed struggle, UP or DOWN, Win or Lose, winner take all. It is a simplistic measuring device, but everything else is so goddam complicated. With one field goal or home run or 3-point shot, we can restore our flagging self-image and get our lives out of the dumpster. We can be on the winning side. The sun will shine again. The world will be a wonderful place. There is cause to celebrate. There is reason to get drunk and overturn police cars.

Losing on the other hand can be dark and angry. If you thought you were going to win, it is an unfair world gone horribly wrong. If you expected to lose, it is a humorless, joyless world. It is a world without hope, full of frustration and bias and incompetence. There is cause to riot. There is reason to get drunk and overturn police cars.

Well it turns out that, from a Dad's perspective, defining "winning" is not so clear-cut. I would like my sons to win on the scoreboard. Every game. Because it feels so good. But what I want even more is for them to know the joy of playing well and the thrill of competition. Competition is after all what drives us, what urges us to become stronger, faster, smarter, quicker. It stimulates our adrenal glands and allows us to do things we didn't know we could do. What a rush that is! I want them to understand good teamwork, pride in effort and the beauty of intensity. All those things.

I remember when a baseball coach of Caleb's, whom I respected a lot, yelled at one of his players for lobbing a ball over to 1st base. It was late in a very long game, and everybody just wanted to go home. "Work on your GAME, son!" he bellowed. For some reason, that stuck in my head. And it's still there. We lost a lot of games that year, but that became our mantra, Caleb's and mine. I realized that the whole point of the season was to get better. At any rate, that's the way I wound up spinning it to Beau. His job is to get better–to improve his skills and his conditioning, to hone his leadership abilities and to try to help his teammates get better.

It turns out winning ain't the only thing. It feels darn good, and it beats the hell out of losing. But it's not even the point really. Winning, as I now see it, has less to do with the outcome than the contest itself. I hold that games are all about reaching, and included in that are concentration and effort and endurance. The point is to get stronger, smarter, faster. The point is to get better. You see, the score may be what you hang your hat on, but it's not where you put your honor.

V

Unanswerable Questions

V

Unanswerable Questions

W. K. Haydon

Uncle Larry's Holiday Wish

...in which Uncle Duke recalls his role model.

Uncle Larry, my mother's brother, had long been a notable eccentric in town. That is to say that he confounded most and disgusted the rest. "A sandwich short of a picnic," they'd whisper. In truth his basket wasn't absolutely full, but what he did have in there was first-rate.

He never had what you'd call a real job. The family pretty much took care of him. Daddy used to say that Larry lived by his wits, but it was only a part-time job. Part of the problem was that his language wasn't fit for polite society. Most of the time it was pushing the outer limits of impolite society. My mother's family had finally given up reforming him. He liked the guttural ring of those words and you couldn't take them away from him. That was that.

Uncle Larry wasn't a total idiot, but he was as close as we came in those parts. This is not to say that he was unintelligent. He was not. He was the best chess player in three counties. He once played a Grand Master in Lexington to a draw. The guy was playing 11 other games at the same time, but still... Not bad for a guy who taught himself. No, he wasn't stupid. His thought processes just followed different paths.

He was definitely good company. Some of the most useful things I know came from Uncle Larry. Such as how to make good pee-in-the-snow art. It's not as easy as it sounds. You can't just go out and start squirting in little circles or run around leaving tracks in big fields of fresh snow. Your footprints will botch it all up. It's best to make geometric shapes and hop from foot to foot so the footprints are part of the pattern. Or stand on a stump and make spinning spirals around it.

Then there was the signature. Good timing was essential to a good, legible signature–good timing and knowing your equipment. Heck, my handwriting got to be better in the snow than it was on paper.

Larry explained that One-A-Day Vitamins made your pee a great neon yellow color. So at the first hint of snow, we'd take mega-doses of vitamin C. He told us that iced tea and warm apple cider gave the longest uninterrupted runs. He was right. Uncle Larry had scientifically researched all of this.

126

Well, after I left town, Larry got older–in a hurry. Though he was not particularly old, his memory, which had always been highly selective, ceased to function. Though his recollection of profanity remained strong, he had no idea who any of us were and referred to us all as different characters from Looney Tunes Cartoons, his favorite TV show. Daddy was always Porky, my mother was Petunia, and I was consistently Daffy. I was flattered. He always liked Daffy best.

Though his speech was often entertaining, it didn't make a whole lot of sense. No sentence ever went with the one that preceded it, or really even made sense on its own. He took to interjecting "Merry Fucking Christmas" at regular intervals. He'd do this year round. If you asked him a question, the answer never even vaguely referred to the question. To say that we talked to Uncle Larry was kind of an exaggeration. In reality, he rambled on like a drunken stevedore, and we mostly just shook our heads. But he seemed happy enough. He ate well. We'd dress him up and take him to major social events in town–mostly funerals, but some weddings too.

So at Cousin Evelyn's wedding when I saw Uncle Larry in an animated conversation with Ed Pinkston, a retired, church-going farmer, I was taken aback. They were having a rousing discussion over by the punch bowl about I-couldn't-imagine-what. Band or no band, they yakked on– expletives, I assumed, undeleted. Whatever it was they were talking about, they talked it up one side and down the other. Maybe Mr. Pinkston had broken the code.

When I finally caught up with my mother and asked her what she figured they were going on about, she threw her head back and laughed. "Oh, Eddie Pinkston's deaf as a post. Spent all those years on a tractor and now he can't hear a train whistle. They're a perfect match. Uncle Larry doesn't make any sense, and Eddie can't tell the difference. There's plenty going out, but nothing's going in."

We paired them up as often as we could after that. I think they were both glad to have the company. "Merry Fucking Christmas," Larry'd say. And a Happy Fucking New Year yourself, Uncle Larry.

Faith of My Fathers

...in which Uncle Duke looks at both sides of the Clergy.

I was born Catholic. Raised Catholic. It was the Faith of my parents and their parents before them. They carried it with them like the family name–with pride and singular devotion. I in turn took it as my own. I memorized the Catechism, learned Latin, served Masses. I marched in innumerable grade school processions, went on retreats, bought Pagan babies and sang hymns piously, if poorly. My family fasted during Lent, ate fish sticks on Fridays and feasted at parish picnics. We said the Rosary every night and went to Confession every Saturday. In short, I believed and worshipped the Catholic God. My Catholic credentials are in order.

But over time, I began to see cracks in the Roman Foundation. It seemed to me that the Church, like all other religions, was less an institution founded and directed by God than an organization, a corporation, founded and directed by Men. Which was not necessarily a bad thing. It just wasn't what It purported to be. So we divorced. Though it was an amicable divorce. We're still friends.

Although I no longer practice the religion, in all likelihood I will die a Catholic. It is like your native tongue. You can learn to speak other languages, but the original lilts and nuances and the inflections of your parents' language are always there. You may say you're no longer Catholic, but the ritual and the ceremony, the celebration and the music of the Church are forever part of you.

It is an impressive organization, the Church. It has persevered for over 2000 years, through profound political and sociological tumult. For all its faults, St. Peter's Rock has proven to be deep and strong and broad based.

From a secular perspective, a worldwide religion is a very labor-intensive business. It is not unlike a military organization. It requires dedicated, lifelong servants. It requires people one can send out into the field and trust to carry out The Mission, intelligent people with imagination and independence, guided by Faith. The Catholic Church has always relied upon individuals who are willing to devote their lives to Its service.

I was taught by a succession of such people–men and women draped in black and white. Dominicans, Xaverians, Jesuits, Franciscans They gave up the popular plumage and a more mainstream life for a Higher Cause. Dressed in cassocks and habits and cinched with rosary beads, they guided and befriended and instructed me well. It was an education that was less about doctrine and theology than method and thought. By turn they were stern and demanding, gentle and understanding. They were dedicated teachers and selfless ministers to whom I am deeply indebted. I have not one unfortunate tale to tell. My feeling is that I am in the majority, that millions of people have been served in the spirit of the Faith and the letter of Canon Law. We have been privileged by their administration.

The clergy indeed has always offered a noble mission. In generations passed, it was considered "The Call". A Vocation meant a Religious Vocation. In the Catholic community, all others were just jobs, ways of supporting a family, making a living. Entering the priesthood in particular was the mark of being hand picked by God to do His earthly work. They did not choose Him. He chose them–to lead the flock, to minister to the congregation. The Call carried with it the respect and admiration of people in and out of the Catholic Church.

Priests and religious have historically been our holy shadows, rebuking temptations and fencing with evil and all its manifestations at every turn. The Roman Collar itself was kind of like Superman's cape. It was bulletproof. No Devil's work could continue for long around it. It was impregnable to the forces of evil, even human ones. Friends of mine doing social work in the hellhole slums of the 60's wore The Collar to avoid the hassles and mayhem they would have normally encountered. It was a white flag in a war zone and engendered universal neutrality, if not respect.

In our own community, we elevated the Clergy to saintly levels. Being somehow nearer to God, they were believed privy to Divine interpretations of things temporal. After all, praying was their job. They talked to God for a living. He was, like, their Boss.

The Catholic religious life has always entailed the emotional sacrifice of wife, children, even family. It requires the ultimate cultural and social sacrifice–the denial of mates and lovers, of intimacy itself. It is the denunciation of an entire dimension of human existence, a dimension many of us consider primary. From an efficiency standpoint, it makes perfect policy sense. All that time normally devoted to wives and kids and the pressures of making a living can now be transferred to the care and nurturing of congregations, a broader family for whom the Priest is the spiritual Father. There are immense benefits. But there are also inevitable costs. There is a potential price to be paid for such personal detachment.

Now it appears that there are those who have violated that trust, who in the most egregious manner used inherited power and respect for their own purposes. It is a sin of unspeakable magnitude. It is a crime which has disfigured and disabled innumerable blameless souls. If one combines the sexual victim, the victim's family, the years of suppression, and in some cases the subsequent victims of these victims, it just becomes incomprehensibly sad. For everyone involved. And even those uninvolved–that large majority of priests and religious who served so well, whose reputations have been besmirched by association. And those parishioner and students whose perception is now clouded by doubt. The sadness is immense and overwhelming.

But it does not end there. Even without the victims themselves, there is a world of pain here. I can imagine the immense guilt and the sense of unforgivable sin carried around in the person of men respected and trusted and loved. They had taken vows of chastity and obedience and had promised to dedicate their lives to the service of the Lord and His people. And in my mind, these were sincere and honest vows. They had hoped to suppress these unconscionable urges within the religious life. But these were men with powerful, all-encompassing desires and, finally, unfortunate opportunity. These were terribly conflicted men with ghastly dark sides and unspeakable secrets.

In the current Church, forgiveness and compassion outrank vengeance and punishment. Ours is mostly a New Testament God. He is not about smiting and casting out into the Wilderness. Given this commitment to amnesty, it does not surprise me that the Church forgave, rehabbed and reassigned. More aware than most of the nature of sin, they were reluctant to cast the first stone. But this is an ignominious and persistent illness. Unfortunately, they didn't understand the Nature of this Beast.

Throughout the Ages, we have traditionally endowed our clergy with strengths and wisdom beyond our own. But it is apparent that the extent to which we as a Culture are flawed is by and large the extent to which the Clergy will be flawed. With the same extremes. And History has proven this so. The Ecclesiastical Record is rife with these excesses and enigmas–holy, devoted men and saintly women with huge, gaping blind spots and brilliant, charismatic Popes with big, ugly axes to grind. We forget that training and title do not necessarily translate into virtue. Neither a prefix nor a suffix is an assurance of character or self-restraint. We fail to remember that respect and prestige, in the wrong hands, can be dangerous opportunities. Even a Roman collar is no guarantee against frailty. What we ignore, at our own peril, is the primary rule of humanity– that we are in fact all most blessedly and fatally human.

"Robust Young Life Closes"

...in which Uncle Duke laments cruel Fate.

I was reminded lately of my long departed uncle, George Lloyd Haydon, Jr. I think it had to do with Veterans' Day, seeing pictures of all those solitary crosses in graveyards across America and elsewhere. All those forgotten souls from long ago battles and disremembered conflicts, laid side by side in silent repose. They all had stories, once upon a time. But we don't know them anymore. And for some reason I thought of my uncle. I had long seen his tombstone in the Haydon plot in the Springfield cemetery. Without much notice, I might add. It is a low, unassuming headstone with simply his name, his years of birth and death (1899-1918) and the place of his death, Ft. Buell, Ky. It is a sad story.

I never knew him, of course. Don't know much about him now. But I always heard of him referred to as "the pick of the litter"– the biggest and strongest, the handsomest and perhaps the smartest of the Haydon lot. He was certainly the heir apparent, his father's name in place. The above title– *A Robust Life Closes*–headed his obituary in the Springfield Sun. And indeed the article refers to him as "the perfect specimen of manhood. 'Jelly' as he was familiarly known (presumably due to his initials–G. L.) was one of the best known young men of the town, and thru his manly bearing had won the affection of all with whom he came into contact." Pretty impressive description, even discounting the florid prose of the time. He was an honor student at Springfield High School and would have graduated in June of 1918 had he remained in school. The details are somewhat blurred here, but it appears that he enlisted in the equivalent of ROTC at the University of Kentucky, which was then Kentucky State College prior to his high school graduation. World War I was in its final stages then, and the assumption is that he wanted to do his part, to test his metal, to get 'over there' and into the fray.

As it turned out, the eager young man with the winning smile and the pleasing personality never got out of his own state. In the Fall of that year, he contracted influenza, the dreaded Spanish flu which decimated whole populations of mostly young and healthy people all across the globe. The flu led to pneumonia from which he did not recover. He went from the picture of health to the grave in less than two weeks.

The family story is that Grandma and Grandpa Haydon went down to the Lexington military hospital, along with the family doctor. But by the time they got there, there was nothing to be done. And indeed the obituary bears this out. "His parents, along with Dr. J. C. Mudd, were at the bedside when the end came." He was 18 years old. History can surely break your heart.

Of course there was a grand wake. He was genuinely and profoundly bereaved. "The body was brought to the home of his parents, Mr. and Mrs. G. L. Haydon that evening, where it was viewed by hundreds of sorrowing relatives and friends, many of whom came from a distance, to pay their last respects to this noble young man, whose death has cast a gloom over the entire community." There was a profusion of beautiful floral designs, a High Mass, dozens of pallbearers and honorary pallbearers marching in formation. And full military honors at the cemetery. It was an heroic funeral for a young man who had done nothing heroic, who had not yet had the chance.

The obituary concludes: "His gentlemanly bearing had made an everlasting impression for good upon all those with whom he came into contact. Therefore pleasant memories of him shall ever linger round the hearthstone from which he has departed." This is what one says at these moments. It is the proper protocol. But it is of course not true. No memories yet linger there. Everyone who knew him has departed as well and taken their stories with them. There remains only the grave marker and some archived small town newspaper clippings. And that fate pretty much awaits all of us unless we are Beethoven or Attila the Hun or Elvis. Someone of note. Our stories get swallowed by Time. Two generations, perhaps three, and we are fortunate if even our names and dates survive. So I pass along my Uncle Jelly's story. Or what remains of it. For posterity's sake. It is my gift to him. The gift of the Living. Because it is all just One Grand Story after all. It can be an heroic story if we get the chance, but most often it is less than that. Pleasant enough memories around the hearthstone, to be sure.

Notes on the Bodhisattva Path

...in which Uncle Duke has a change of heart.

I was asked to pick up two dogs from the clinic near my house last week and transport them out to Warren Co. for the daughter of a friend. They had been to the "Quick Fix" Clinic and had their reproductive lives cut short. They'd spent the night in the pens there and were slightly disoriented and a little agog when I picked them up. It was a warm enough week, and all I wanted to do was to have them deposited in the back of my truck so I would then not have my privacy disturbed by any four-legged, whiny fur-ball. The only animals I care much about are my own. And then, not always. I was an over-the-road truck driver, transporting product. My contract did not stipulate interaction with said product. Pick up and deliver. That was the deal.

Somehow, things seldom go according to plan. I got there late and the place was packed with people and their animals. Anxious, loud animals and anxious, loud people and the smell of animal piss with a touch of hysteria. I shoulder through to pick up my cargo and get a long and detailed instruction from one of the puppy-huggers there on "the care and maintenance of post-surgical dogs". "Not my problem," I mumble. "I'm a truck driver." She gives me the instructions anyway. Twice, I think. Because she could tell I wasn't really paying attention.

There is one dog yapping incessantly in the back. "That's Copper," she says. "He's ready to go home." "Great," I think. "A yapper. But at least he'll be in the bed of the truck."

So they bring out Copper and Daisy, my charges, and I try to put them in their carrying cages. Not as easy as you might think. I'm outside the terms of my contract, but I do it anyway so that I can get me and my cargo on the road. But when I go to lift Copper's cage, the top pulls apart from the bottom. "Not good," say the attendants. I grab Daisy's cage and the two of them muscle the other cage with Copper in it out to my truck. I put them both in the back. "You can't put Copper back there," both puppy-huggers now say. "The cage can pull apart and he could wind up on the highway." "It'll be fine," I say. "I've got rope. I'll tie it down." "No, the door to the cage could fly open," they say. "Fine," I say, not meaning anything at all like 'Fine'. At this point, I can't say that the welfare of this animal is high on my agenda. This dog had become an aggravation, seriously interfering with my day.

So we wedge the cage into my passenger seat and shove the door closed. I get in and pull out. I am on the road at last. But now I have a cab-in-mate. He is a Beagle. I've never cared for Beagles. Don't much like short-haired, smallish dogs. They annoy me. He moans, low and long.

I speak to him, my teeth clenched, through the bars of the cage: "Look here, Jughead. Neither of us asked for any of this. Let's just try to make the best of it, OK?"

And that dog looks up at me with the saddest damn eyes I have ever seen in my life. They are shifting back and forth. There is both sorrow and unadulterated terror in those eyes. Fear and trepidation. He has had some pretty weird human shit done to him in the last 24 hours, and it is obvious that he is pretty sure he is going to die today. He doesn't know me but assumes that I am a dog slaver. Or a serial puppy killer. And I admit I have done nothing to make him think anything different.

In either case, he believes that the safe and secure world that he has known for most of his life is behind him. Gone. I am his future, he believes. And I have the distinctive, pungent odor of a Beagle torturer. I look at those eyes again, and in a moment, I realize that THIS is Suffering.

◆ ◆ ◆

Now, I am pretty much a Buddhist these days. Not a very good one, but as good a one as I know how to be. I _do_ practice. And a major component of what Buddhists believe is that all of us living and breathing things Suffer. Not all of the time, but enough that we spend a lot of our time and energy trying NOT to suffer. It is called _dukkha_. It is a Sanskrit term, and I've always thought it was the perfect word/sound for that low and mournful and unrelenting pain that is Suffering. And Copper was, at that moment, up to his brown eye-balls in a full-blown, universal case of dukkha.

I have looked out at the World through those eyes and moaned long and low myself. I understand his Fear. It is that nowhere-to-hide fear against which we are seemingly powerless. It is that all-consuming fear that makes it difficult to think or even breathe. It is that overwhelming fear that we would do anything to rid ourselves of. I know it well.

And one of the primary goals of Buddhism is not only to come to grips with our own suffering, but to help other beings overcome theirs. It is called the Bodhisattva Path. There are vows to that effect, and I have in fact taken them. And suddenly I understand that it is my immediate job, here and now, to help young Mr. Copper to diminish his intense suffering. As best I can.

So I take a deep breath. I relax my shoulders. My tone changes, and I begin to talk to him, as soothingly as I can, about his life. I tell him that it is NOT over. That he WILL see his family again. I promise to deliver him. Soon. He is fine, I say. He's just hungry and uncomfortable and a little hung over. I gently break the news to him that there won't be any Copper Juniors in his future. But I tell him that he is still a young pup, and that he will have many days ahead and lots of rabbits to chase and squirrels to bark at and whole forests of trees to pee on and probably puppy chow to his heart's content. And then I tell him that sex is overrated anyhow. I lied about that. But the truth is generally best meted out in small portions.

But I proceed to spend the rest of the trip explaining to him what I know about Buddhism. Because he looked like he might be interested. I start with the Four Noble Truths, but I don't get far because they're hard to explain to a Beagle without the basic teachings. Dogs don't pick up Sanskrit very quickly, and my own understanding and ability to explain is pretty limited. But I do my best, and he seems to appreciate the effort.

When we are almost there, I reach down with one hand for him to sniff. He does, and he looks at me. With a wonderfully calm and steady gaze. His eyes are deep and brown and trusting. And, it seems, kind of grateful.

Apparently there is this thing called compassion. I had heard of it as a younger man but was not really familiar with it. It turns out that we are, all of us, sometimes capable of it. Even despite our worst intentions. It does not appear to be our natural state, but it is in fact learnable. Under the right conditions, we can teach each other.

The Other Side of the Street

…in which Uncle Duke looks at a different path.

I'm not sure what all this fuss is about homosexuality. It strikes me as a rather straight-forward matter actually, vastly over-complicated by a culture with an over-simplified moral outlook and a figuratively clenched butt. In my view, God doesn't give a fig who you have sex with. Or where you put your do-hickey. Of course I like to think my judgment is uncomplicated by Standard Morals. I am unbound by Biblical pronouncements and religious beliefs. My view of the world is from the Natural Perspective–what we do to adapt, how we respond as a species to changing conditions. Life is mostly a terribly interesting biological experiment as far as I'm concerned.

That said, and given Darwin and all, it is curious to me that men and women would combine in a non-procreative way. I am aware of that happening in the Animal World only in rare instances. And I don't entirely understand those cases. But the whole Human approach to sexuality and sex is so vastly different from any other natural species. Our mating season is January 1 to January 1. 24/7. In the 21st Century, sex is more and more about pleasure and power and less and less about procreation. The link is tenuous at best. In the rest of the Animal Kingdom, successful mating produces fertilized eggs followed by newborns. In the Human Kingdom, mostly it does not. If I were to estimate the percentage of sexual acts each day which had the intention of creating an offspring…Well, the number would be small. We time estrus, block our own inseminating fluids and take pills designed to fool our bodies, all in order to prevent procreation, to control birth. In the history of the world, Folks, this behavior is absolutely unique.

The regulating internal command in the Natural World has always been to put out as many little copies of ourselves as possible without dying in the process. The reproductive maxim has been to overwhelm the predators, larger and faster than ourselves, with sheer numbers. If our progeny didn't starve or get eaten, we were successful.

Well, due to our unprecedented reproductive success, which produced an overwhelming flood of humanity, and aided by personal Weapons of

Mass Destruction, the predators are hanging on by their claws. They are pacing back and forth in teeny little parks and preserves, being photographed all the livelong day. They lost. We grow other animals for them to eat. We won.

So survival-wise, there is really not that much of an imperative to go out there and breed. Even so, it has always been seen as a moral imperative to populate the world. We were expected to sow our seed broadly. It was some kind of solemn obligation to spread ourselves and our genes, our cultures and our religions, far and wide. So the procreative dance went on out of a sense of duty.

And there is still a lot of that going on. Some people think the goal is to outnumber the enemy, whomever we perceive that to be. Well, it turns out that sheer numbers do not win wars any longer– militarily or culturally. And actually, overly large populations are a threat to governments and cultures around the world. It turns out we have to find something for those people to do. We have to supply them with jobs which require resources, both natural and human.

The long and short of it is, we have enough people. Way enough. Dare I say a surfeit. So it doesn't surprise me that men and women are pairing for other reasons. Without regard for regeneration. If amphibians can physically change sexes in response to environmental pressures, then surely humans can change sexual preference in response to population pressures.

And I am not offended or angered by this. The fewer breeders the better, I say. I am offended and angered, on the other hand, by couples or individuals who continue to pound out large litters of children in the face of a burgeoning World population. I view that as irresponsible. That's about as close to moral indignation as I get.

Now, unless I am misreading the anecdotal evidence, homosexuality is by and large not a chosen lifestyle. If anything, the tendency is persistently denied and fiercely resisted–often to an unhealthy extent. And no wonder. Objects of ridicule and scorn, subject to prejudice, intimidation and bullying, who would choose to be gay? For most of our History, they have been unwelcome aliens. In an overwhelming majority of the planet, they are still persecuted and despised. "Ooo-Kaaay. That sounds like fun. I think I'll be gay." Well to me it sounds more like an act of self-affirming bravery actually. Or am I over-romanticizing something that people do just

W. K. Haydon

to stay alive? I do that sometimes.

The Culture takes a curious stance on this issue. It does a lot of finger-pointing and legislating. To me, that is akin to blaming and shaming and prosecuting those born left-handed. We can force people to use their right hands. Indeed we consistently did that not very long ago. But that takes a lot of time and energy. And in the end, it makes for a pretty lousy right-hander. And we already have a lot of lousy heterosexuals. So why make more? We also tried shaming people for being born Black, and Red, and Yellow. But it only made dispirited and angry non-White persons. Shaming people into a false lifestyle has proved to be an inefficient and unsuccessful tactic. It diminishes all involved and changes nothing. You can look it up.

It is curious to me how views change so markedly when "real" families have "real" homosexuals born in their midst. When a cherished face and a known history are combined with a dreaded, feared word, there is generally a progression that goes on in that family. It is often painful, but eventually doctrines crumble, rigidity dissipates, anger allays. The softening that goes on in that family is the softening that will in time take place in our Culture. I am confident of that. Letting go of our Fear is the first step. Embracing those figurative left-handers out there is next.

I have, of course, thought about my own children. How would I react? Would my acceptance be as wide and encompassing as I'd like to believe? How big is my tent? Would I welcome a boy friend to Thanksgiving Dinner with the same warmth as I would a girl friend? What about public displays of affection–hand-holding on the street, nuzzling in the TV room? What about shared bedrooms and all those questions? I'd need to undergo some major shifts in my working model, that's for sure. I'd have some work to do.

And I have to say, I would be afraid. For them, mostly. No one wants their children to spend their lives swimming upstream. To be homosexual, even now, is to continually struggle against a prevailing, persistent current. First, there is the difficult struggle to realize who you are. Then I imagine the fierce, see-saw battle for self-acceptance. Then, there begins the life-long battle of living in the counter culture. It's a hard row to hoe. I'd like my sons to waltz through life, not push big, old boulders up long, steep hills. But yes, I'm confident I could adjust. If I had to. Love, I trust, would overwhelm me.

139

And it's all about love. Love and Compassion. It's not at all complicated really. There is such a preponderance of fear and anger out there. It strikes me that wherever we find love and respect, we have the obligation to nurture it. Whenever we find sane, supportive caregivers to raise children, run scout troops or lead congregations, we should encourage them. In my view, all human relationships boil down to love and respect. Superficial relationships are just that–gay or straight. Promiscuity is just as risky and unhealthy among heterosexuals as homosexuals. Commitment and responsibility in relationships are just as laudable and beneficial to the culture among Lesbians as among Mormons. Or Cowboys. Or Tuba Players. I make no distinction.

So whenever two individuals are willing to commit to each other, to pledge their troth, what is the harm? We all gain. And there are millions of children out there birthed without love or affection, direction or respect. The World begs for intelligent parents. What loving Lord would object? Certainly not mine. I know. I have discussed this with God on a number of occasions. And She was very clear on this. There is but one rule: Be Kind to One Another.

Country Boys, Friday Night

…in which Uncle Duke and his father explore the Big City.

When it came to bourbon, my father knew what he liked. There was of course an age requirement. 8-Years-Old was a respectful minimum. Anything less than that was rather like asking a boy to do a man's job. And 100 proof was certainly a desirable quality. If for no other reason, anything less than 100 was imperfect at the base of it, so why bother.

Also, he was not blind to packaging. An attractive or unique bottle was certainly a point in its favor. And lastly, he was rigidly parochial in his taste. To my knowledge, he never bought a bottle of bourbon distilled outside of Nelson County, Kentucky. There were territorial and familial allegiances to be observed, after all.

So for him, buying a bottle of bourbon was like buying a suit. It was a major, long-term investment, one that you had to live with, one which required forethought and complete knowledge of the product.

Thus it did not surprise me on a Friday night at the old 9-0-5 liquor store on Hampton, on one of his infrequent trips to St. Louis, when my father attempted to engage a clerk there in a question and answer session on the finer points of some of his shelf whiskey.

"What do you have in a green label," he asked, referring to the green tax stamp signifying 100 proof. This was a question anyone the age of young bourbon could answer in Kentucky. This guy however waved lamely at a bottle of scotch which happened to be wrapped in green. Daddy looked at me with his look which said: "You live here?" The clerk was doing his best, but he was uneducated and unused to doing anything more than reading labels and making change. And he saw, as I did, that there was a steadily lengthening line of some seriously thirsty patrons behind us, anxious to begin their weekend debauchery. Sentiment was about evenly divided at this time about who to blame for the holdup, the management or the old guy with the accent.

Daddy was quite unaware. I'm not sure it would have mattered if he were. After all, no one rushed you when you were buying a washing machine, and they were mostly all the same. He was considering bourbon here. This was pretty near a marriage, not some silly one-night stand with sloe gin or malt liquor. He was concentrating, for God's sake.

"Got any Old McKenna centennial bottles?" he inquired. The poor man's eyes raced wildly around the store for a bottle to get him off the hook. He inadvisably pointed to a bottle of vodka shaped like a potato. Daddy was becoming exasperated. His respect for St. Louisans was crumbling fast. In fact his confidence in the entire state of Missouri was in a rather rapid decline. If the sales staff at a prominent liquor store had so little knowledge of its product and so little time for interested customers, why he didn't foresee ever buying any appliances west of the Mississippi.

The situation was becoming dangerous as the line grew longer and more demanding. Several had opened their purchases and gave every indication that they would entirely consume them before they paid for them, setting up a rather prickly customer relations problem for a clerk whose public relations were already in serious disrepair.

Daddy showed no sign of compromise. Looking back, I do not recall that being one of his strong suits. He was however aware of timetables, and we were rapidly getting behinder in ours. I suggested that, under the circumstances, Jim Beam was a reliable brand, one in which my grandfather himself had expressed a great deal of confidence. I offered further that I didn't think I'd ever seen it in one of those guitar-shaped bottles before. The hubbub behind us was now quite audible and even Daddy realized that this was a crisis that could use some defusing. So we made our purchase, thanked the clerk for his enlightened assistance and left the premises.

I have thought of that evening more than once. Whenever I do, my respect for my father grows. He had earned his money, he wanted equal value for it and, by God, no crowd of Friday-night Missouri boneheads was going to deter him.

It is true. He could aggravate me to death. In fact, nobody was ever better at it. But I have to say that, by and large, my mother married well.

Capitalism Rules

...in which Uncle Duke learns to embrace an old Enemy.

I will say this for Capitalism. It trumps Ideology. And since I've about had it up to my earlobes in Ideology, I've become a big Capitalist fan. It's a pretty cut and dried system. The Customer Rules. Capitalism is mostly a non-judgmental enterprise. Or if you have a judgment, you keep it to yourself as you make the sale. Your ideology won't pay the rent. Gays and lesbians need not worry about being turned away at a Ford dealership. Jews, Christians, Atheists, Moslems, even Buddhists are welcome at Best Buy. All colors and manners of people can shop til they drop at Home Depot. Retailers will sell to whoever walks in the door as long as their credit is good. Bring us all your tired, your wrinkled, your sweat-stained, moldy, contaminated money. We will accept it just like any other.

And I praise them for this. This is not Political Correctness. It is the correctness of 'money talks'. This is not subjective altruism but pure and simple, bottom line math. It is a profit and loss statement. Customers are 'profit' and being seen as intolerant, particularly to a changing demographic is 'loss'. Today's underclass is tomorrow's customer. So if I offend you today, it is not likely you will buy my Brand tomorrow. And if I tolerate those who offend you, it will be remembered. It doesn't matter if I understand or agree or disagree with whatever it is that offends you. Apologizing for offending someone is not a matter of 'political correctness'. It is a matter of Economics. "Hey, Get Over It!" is an incorrect response. Being polite to people is good business. Listening to ALL people, being nice to ALL people gives you an economic advantage. Politicians and preachers can insult all manners of people outside their parties and congregations and somehow get away with it. Merchants don't have that luxury. They need more than a simple majority. They need as many customers as they can get.

Now one could say that that is not a valid reason for kindness. Even politeness. Businesses are after all not really people. So it's not quite a human emotion, a real response to someone else's pain or discomfort. But it's close enough. It's almost empathy and not far from compassion, in a dollars-and-cents sort of way. Whatever. I salute you, Capitalism. All hail the great Social and Political Equalizer.

You saw the way those Big Box stores unloaded the Confederate flag. They have people on staff who could tell you to about six decimal places what keeping that flag on their shelves would have cost them. So they deliberated...oh say, 10 minutes. They understand who butters their bread.

NASCAR, that entity that I had always despised for its shameless capitalist pandering, its plentiful-and-crowded company logo patches, was more than willing to ditch and dispense the Confederate flag once it saw that adherence to it could harm its Brand. And good on you, NASCAR, I say. It was a dollars and sense decision based on the potential to expand markets and keep Advertisers happy. And Advertisers are happy when their customers are happy. And they want EVERYBODY to be a Customer someday. This was GOOD pandering. Symbols come and go, but Customers keep those engines running.

South Carolina could also see that that flag was an Old South anchor it was dragging around. It was damaging its image and thereby impeding its future business and investment potential. It had been looking to unhitch itself from that ante-bellum, cracker icon for some time now. That night-riding holdover flag was bad business ju-ju. And good on you too, South Carolina, for showing a solid grasp of the Market Economy. Congratulations for recognizing the value of inclusiveness, which translates to expanding opportunities. The Ethics of this whole situation will perhaps come along later.

On other fronts, the Capitalists of America are lined up and chomping at the bit to get to that Caribbean Evil Empire, that Communist Den of Iniquity, Cuba. Christian customers, Commie customers–Who Cares??? C-U-S-T-O-M-E-R-S, by God. Goods-deprived, consumption-starved, money-in-their-pockets, Spanish speaking customers can damn well buy our products and who gives three hoots for ideology or politics or even theology for God sakes. The boats are booked and packed with goodies to lure those pesos out of their mattresses. We let bygones be bygones and by the way if you buy a dozen we'll take off 10%. There will soon be Capitalists swimming to Cuba with product on their backs. To be first on the beach and have a crack at that new source of revenue. To paraphrase Michael Jordan: "Communists buy sneakers too, you know." Wa-fucking-hoo. New Markets!!!

The Capitalists did go a little overboard in the previous decade. They got a little too egalitarian. In its blind pursuit of personal wealth (It is prone to do that.) the System utilized poor business practices to make bad loans to both Rich AND Poor people. It was an equal opportunity fuck-up. Of course the Poor and Middle Class got hurt more because they had no nest egg, nothing to fall back on. But I was encouraged to realize that Greed does not discriminate. It will in fact, all things being equal, target the Rich when possible because they have more to contribute. Though they also can afford better lawyers.

We all understand it's an imperfect system. People get left behind. Bad things happen to good people. But to my mind Capitalism is more likely to throw open its doors and let people in than a fair number of churches and certain political parties. Because no one is in business to get smaller, eh. And customers come in all shapes, sizes, colors and persuasions. You pay your nickel and, pretty much, they let you in the door.

A Second Chance at the Seventh Grade

...in which Uncle Duke goes back to school.

I am being required to retake the seventh grade this year. There are a number of reasons. One of the most prominent of which is that during most of my adolescence, I suffered from an attention deficit. This was not so much a certifiable disorder as it was a protective condition. I can still recall the sound of adults talking to me. I saw their lips move very clearly, but what came out of their mouths was muffled and garbled. I could hear my friends well enough; but with grown-ups, it was like one of us was under water. I suppose that would have been me. My brain seemed surrounded by a semi-permeable, viscous cushion. As I look back, it was there to provide a barrier, an effective baffle, between me and a lot of confusing, contradictory stuff.

In case you've forgotten, there is an overwhelming amount of information out there for twelve year olds. Everybody has information for you to absorb, rules for you to memorize, lessons to teach you and things for you to remember. Most of it is redundant, but never mind. It's all terribly important stuff, and it will most certainly ruin your life if you don't remember it.

The brain, we know, is an amazing organism, capable of incredible feats of calculation and absorption. But it has its limits. There are things it refuses to do. The first time we are exposed to information or facts, particularly when we are not ready for them, our brains reject them like some alien, invading organism. It protects itself from overload, particularly in our formative years, by blocking out extraneous, unnecessary information. In my case, this was History, Geography and most areas of Science.

However, it turns out that one cannot be exposed to words and phrases dozens of times without them being reluctantly imprinted in some backwater node of the brain. As a result there are loose pieces of information which rattle around in our brains for years, like pebbles in a hubcap. What was that Magna Charta thing? Who the hell was Cardinal Richelieu and why does he pop into my head more often than truly significant historical figures like The Big Bopper and Little Richard? We wander around most of our lives with something called the Hawley-Smoot Tariff tucked into our brains and no support information. It doesn't keep us awake at night, but it is a significant void.

Let me say here that I think I know enough stuff. I have accumulated quite a lot of information already in one lifetime and am just about as smart as I care to be. In some areas I have way more information than I need. I just need to fill in the gaps of the stuff that's already in my brain and I will be just-smart-enough.

I am not, at this point, interested in scholarly works. I was always a Cliff Notes kind of guy anyway. Historically, one 3-4 page chapter for about every twenty years or so is about right. I don't want to be weighted down with the specifics of one generation of history or one scientific phenomenon or another. I want The Big Picture. I want a real Liberal Arts education. I want The Seventh Grade.

Well it turns out, to my wonderful surprise, that information is tastier and more compelling the second time around. It turns out that this is terribly interesting stuff. World War I was an intricate series of political, ethnic, geographical and economic events with subplots of greed, vanity and lust. Who knew? All of a sudden, in my middle years, a history textbook reads like a novel. Somehow I involuntarily absorbed enough information over the years to provide a solid framework for 7th grade class work. I get it! Having struggled against gravity, friction and inertia all these years, suddenly the elementary laws of physics and the accompanying equations make sense. Why of course Force = Mass x Acceleration! I knew that! The study of mountain ranges and tectonic plates may be dull and slow moving, but hey!–dull and slow moving is my preferred pace. The Classics may be moldy, but I've grown to *like* moldy. It's a perfect match!

But of course the real reason I'm retaking seventh grade is to walk it with Caleb. I recognize that it's not easy being twelve. Twelve year olds are still learning how to comb their hair and spit properly. Their bodies require a lot of their brains' attention as they pull and stretch and spurt in multiple directions at once. They are paying a lot of attention to chemistry, but it is internal chemistry, not the theoretical kind. The exact formulas are irrelevant.

They are determining how the world works, how to maneuver, go through the gears, get respect, get food, get whatever else they need. This is pretty much a full-time job. To expect them to concentrate on abstract issues and dead people is asking an awful lot. Dead stuff does not register a ping on their screen. Everything is alive and in front of them. This is why they grasp computer technology so readily. It is living, breathing and changing and is basically the same age they are. We ask them to learn LATIN, a language no longer spoken? This is adult logic, which is to say-- it makes no immediate sense.

No sir, seventh grade is not easy. Our memories may distort and rosify it, but there is a lot of new stuff coming at you. A lot of requirements. And they're not always laid out terribly clearly for you. It can be very confusing, even overwhelming. I know Caleb feels trapped and tricked and under-informed on a pretty regular basis. It is the adults' job to help explain the details—what's important, what's not. More importantly, it is our job to supply perspective. Why is it important? Since I wasn't paying much attention the first time through, I don't really know. There's a lot I have to relearn.

He asked me recently to read an assigned novel along with him. The book was Where the Red Fern Grows, and it is about a boy and his two coon dogs. The dogs are of course intelligent and loyal, brave and fierce and play a central role in the boy's adolescent life. They get into trouble, charm everyone, win contests. They learn from him. He learns from them. They save his life. He saves theirs. Eventually, one is killed by a cougar. And shortly thereafter, the other dies of a broken heart.

It was hard. The book had become real, as good literature is supposed to do. We had grown to love those hounds, and we were both terribly saddened by their demise. It was real enough pain. We held each other for a long time.

At that moment, I realized I belonged in the seventh grade. It was where I needed to be. There were some lessons I didn't learn the first time around. How to hold on to a good friend and share a good cry was one of them.

W. K. Haydon

VI

Redemption

A History of S*X, Part II

...in which Uncle Duke peeks at modern sexuality.

It is evident to me that when it comes to sex, we are a nation of adolescents. By and large, we are arrested at the comic book, pajama party stage. As mature adults, we can discuss plumbing, computer files, hard drives, digestive tracts, even reproductive systems, analytically, in exhaustive detail. We can dissect most subjects in the natural world soberly and matter-of-factly. But when the conversation turns to the act itself, putting the round peg in the round hole, when it reverts to those series of events that led to our own bleeping conception, we lock up. We get embarrassed. We squirm and giggle and look for a way out. Mostly we make jokes, which is our way of dancing around uncomfortable issues. Which is why sex is the subject of so many sitcoms and bad movies. We put actors in embarrassing and awkward situations for us so we can safely laugh at their discomfort. Like Race, we don't know how to discuss it honestly, face-to-face, so we try to make it funny and give the lines to actors.

This is not exclusively a "male" issue by the way. I haven't done much hard polling on the issue (under advice of counsel), but it does seem clear that women are almost as titillated and intrigued by the sexual experience as men. From the number of predominantly women's magazines which feature articles on sex and its resultant pleasures and frustrations, I'd say it cuts across gender lines pretty darn completely. Women are more honest, of course. Their discussions are more frank. Their magazines are more factual and descriptive. Women apparently rely much less on pictures in their educational material than men do.

And advertisers certainly cash in on that intrigue. You want titillation, they wrote the book. If they can somehow put us in the sex mode, if they can turn us on, flip our triggers, get us to connect their product with sex in some remote, even obscure way, they are already in our back pockets. We are hooked fish. The ads are blatant, transparent and incredibly effective. The remote freezes in our hands. We don't even struggle. The research is painfully clear on this one. We are absolute and complete suckers for gratuitous sex. The more blatant the better. It is what I term 'tit-for-tat advertising'. They show you a little, stroke your libido, and you will listen to what they have to say and probably buy their brand of whatzit. You can deny the reason if you want, but they can show you the numbers. Can you say P-A-V-L-O-V? Not much has changed over time. Sex was after all the original bartering tool.

Since we have such a long history with sex, there is somehow the illusion that it is instinctual, that it is an elementary physical function. Well, it is and it isn't. While it is true we were born with the urge to mate, sex is seldom simple. It has become terribly complex. This interaction between two people, this interplay between partners, ceased being a simple physical act thousands of generations ago. The mind, the emotions, culture and religion became entangled with the act in our ancient past. It became confused with power, prestige and potency. Sex became Big Medicine.

Which it still is. The ground rules are unwritten, mostly unspoken, and change daily even within established couples. Who leads? Who follows? Which pathways are restricted and which are gardens of delight? There are anomalies and mysteries and subtleties galore. Yet there are no teachers–at least outside of Institutes. Oh sure, you can learn the basic biology of the act, the sexual hydraulics, the plumbing parts in health class. If we want to learn ballroom dancing, French cooking, pipe fitting, wine tasting, martial arts, computer skills, there are classes and seminars out the wazoo. If we want to learn how just about anything works, the subtleties involved, how to refine our skills, you can find a class. Masters will teach you. There are apprenticeship programs. Yet with sex, you pretty much have to learn on your own–trial and error. Mind you, it's not a bad way to learn. On-the-job training is a widely used learning technique in many disciplines. It works pretty well. It's just that there's a lot of wasted time and squandered experiences. As we grope for answers, there's a lot of useless grappling and unnecessary frustration and embarrassment, which sometimes lasts a lifetime. And there are apparently lots of people who never get it. Sex becomes wrapped in ego and memories and guilt and insecurities, accelerated hopes and groundless fears. And much of the richness gets lost. Which is sad.

I blame our previously mentioned unease (or in this case, dis-ease) with the subject. The window for discussion is wide open in adolescence. What do kids really want to know about in high school? Ionic bonds? The principal export of Ecuador? Pythagoras? Of course not. They are cauldrons of hormones with hundreds of really legitimate questions about sex.

Yet we make most of the words needed to talk about it off-limits. Then we build a pretty impenetrable wall around it and make it mysterious enough that advertising and the Internet can then make money providing peepholes into the forbidden zone. They trivialize and objectify it for profit. Then the pornography industry makes billions providing virtual sex in the absence of real intimacy. People selling fantasy are not interested in promoting the self-growth, spirituality and interpersonal communication inherent in sex. For them, the "making love" part just gets in the way.

In other cultures, in periods long past, there were courtesans hired to escort the uninitiated into the hallowed ground. There were teachers who instructed beginners in the science of lovemaking, the art of the kama sutra. It was a system designed to define sexual etiquette, to refine our tastes, and make sex a pleasurable, meaningful act for both parties. Radical, eh?

Actually, for such an essential skill, this sounds pretty reasonable. However, in the absence of such hands-on instruction, perhaps some honesty would help. The wall was put there to make us afraid, to keep us out. But of course all it does is make us curious and open us up to misconceptions, unwanted conceptions, confusion and sexually transmitted diseases. I say, bring it down. Open the gates. Turn on the lights. Sex is not a mountain to climb. It's a beach to lie on.

Yin and Yang

...in which Uncle Duke celebrates Renewal.

Well the Serviceberry and the Red Buds have come and gone, and the Dogwoods are reborn. Hallelujah! The Dog Tooth Violets and Dutchman's Breeches and Bloodroot and May Apples are all alive and well, thank you, basking and soaking up energy so they can later send their little fuzzy-cheeked progeny out into the void to hopefully take hold somewhere and continue the line. There is no shortness of hope this time of year. It pokes out of the ground like mushrooms, fresh for the picking. And there is a sweetness and gentleness in the air in April like there is at no other.

The snakes are out and running. The Black snakes and the Racers, the Kings and the Hognoses are awake and sleek and very hungry. The Copperheads are coiled and patient, while the water snakes slip surreptitiously along the shorelines. I have always admired snakes. They have resisted a civilian army of humans out to get them – old ladies with hoes, kids with ball bats and men with shovels and blades and fat, black tires. Despite a reputation for malevolence that goes clear back to Adam and Eve, they have maintained and even flourished. Anything that moves with that much grace and fluidity deserves my respect, I figure.

And the turtles are back, sojourning unhurriedly from one pointless point on the globe to another, crossing the road for its own sake. There is nothing like a turtle to make one believe in continuity. The plodding, age-less, seemingly dim-witted turtle that dined with dinosaurs and now co-exists with condos.

The other day I came upon an event so touching and poignant, so full of life and hope. I speak of course of the rare and beautiful–turtle love. Turtles make love with such elegance. It is so tender and solemn and si-lent–only the slightest clickety-clack towards the very end. I don't suppose I expected to see a roller-coaster ride or hear moon rockets, but I was sur-prised at how slow it was–like watching the minute hand on a clock. It's like they had expended so much energy just trying to find each other, they wanted to make it last. Despite feeling a twinge of voyeuristic guilt, I felt renewed and enriched by the experience, a feeling I imagine God might feel after overseeing a particularly successful human coitus.

But of course I am only sure that Spring is Spring and all's right with the world when I sight that contented ground hog sunning his big, old wooly self on the boulder at the base of Lake Aspen's levy. Over the years I have named him Gomer and have alternately admired him and hated him – admired him for living so effortlessly off the fat of the land, and hated him for the very same reason, particularly when I have felt beleaguered by the weight of the human condition–mortality, original sin and all that. But by and large I respect him for letting the world come to him and for finding and maintaining this lifestyle-of-least-resistance. And I am glad to see that he survived another Winter.

So I am gladdened by Spring. It is my favorite time of year. But it is a joy that is tempered by Warren's death. Or perhaps the grief of a good friend's passing is tempered by the renewal of Spring. In any case we celebrate the balance. Part of us is always dying, after all, and part is being born. Warren's life passes from us, and the Dogwoods are reborn.

155

A Bourgeoning Beau

...in which Uncle Duke goes eye-ball to eye-ball with an 8th Grader.

It has been my privilege, lo these last 14 years, to be Beau's dad. It has been way cool, and I am for certain a better man for it. It is a task I know how to do. It is a job I am good at. A man's worth is tested in Fatherhood as nothing else.

He is currently in eighth grade–the aptly named 'Middle School'. Poised somewhere between the innocent, soft, round edges of primary school and the harder, more worldly boundaries of high school and beyond, it is a wonderful time to know him.

But it has always been so. From the earliest days, with his pudgy grin and easy disposition, he has always had a presence that is comfortable to be around. "Morning, Beau-ster," I've always said when I wake him up. "How ya' doin'?" "Good," he has always responded, without hesitation. Often still he wakes up singing. There is an optimism there that seldom waivers. It is an honest response to a World that has been good to him.

I love to listen to him play his trumpet. Not that it is necessarily pleasing to the ear. I wouldn't call it that. He is not...(How shall I put this?)...he is not the Second Coming of Miles Davis. His genius likely lies in other areas. The notes are seldom round. 'Lilting' is not a word I would use. They are typically flat, largely discordant and mostly asymmetrical. However, they are also fat and enthusiastic and completely unabashed. They are so damn plump and joyous and full of confidence that you could walk on them, I swear. They barge from room to room and fill the house like bright, slightly misshapen balloons. It is sacred noise, and I am sorry when he stops

I love to fix him breakfast. It is the only meal I am entrusted to make at my house. And in truth, I don't have a lot of range. But then, what does he know from Eggs Benedict? He doesn't have all that much experience out in the world. Dad's breakfast is still the Gold Standard. Anyone can fix him lunch. He can fix his own. But breakfast is Dad's meal. It is the top of the morning, a largely unoccupied time slot. And it is my morning gift to start his day, my protein punch to jump start his brain and keep it functioning throughout the morning. It is a thing of value, and I am proud to give it.

We are in a delightful cusp these days. His voice waivers between two worlds. It is undecided where it belongs. It mostly resides in a profundo pit. It is a thick, masculine molasses that sometimes scares the hell out of me in the hall in the middle of the night. But it often still soars into high innocence at inopportune moments before diving quickly back into his masculine barrel. These are comical moments. It is a humorous little opera, a one-man show of multiple aged characters. The metaphor is so obvious that even he recognizes it and is amused.

He argues with me at every opportunity. And he is not the first person to do so. I admit that my interpretation of the world is subject to some considerable question. And it is true that my memory is unreliable, and that my recollection of the chronology of events and people is continually, within our family, subject to cross examination. But he is certainly the only person (other than Diana perhaps) who does it with such regularity, enthusiasm and out-and-out gusto. I have been flat wrong, and caught at it, enough times for him to know that it's at least even money to pick the other side, to challenge the House. And that is in fact his JOB. It is a form of jousting, I think. Fencing perhaps. It is a form of intellectual and verbal parrying to which 8th grade boys are compelled. But it is an awkward little crossroads. I, at my age, have a vested interest in being RIGHT. A man of my Wisdom and Experience has under his hat vast quantities of TRUTH and INSIGHT and should have stature enough to not be challenged by no BONEHEAD 8TH GRADER WITH BAGGY JEANS AND HIS HAT ON BACKWARDS!!!

But that is indeed the nature of things. We have been put here, he and I, to challenge each other's skills and broaden our abilities to compromise and to expand our understanding and compassion. His job is to expose me to the culture of youth and change. And my job is to expose him to fogey logic. Not that either of us will ever embrace the other's position. God forbid. There are Universal Laws to observe here. But just enough so that we understand that there are semi-human life forms, some of whom we know intimately, that do embrace them.

It is not easy being in the 8th grade. There are opposing forces that tug and pull. Powerful cultural forces. The need to be accepted, part of a group. Those strong, individual genetic forces that want to lead him along roads less traveled and the compelling cultural forces that urge him to conform. There is the awkward biological imperative that urges him away from the nest and parental intimacy, and the simultaneous necessities of pre-drivers license, multiple destinations divided by humongous distances. Compromises need to be made, but compromise is an acquired skill. A lot of 14 year olds burn some pretty strategic bridges without realizing they'll need to cross over them again.

We stand eyeball to eyeball these days. He puffs his bird chest out and cocks his head menacingly. "You wanna go, Old Man?" he sneers. I stare back, curl my lip and do my best Dirty Harry. "You feelin' lucky, Punk?" It is a Mexican standoff. Nose to nose, we stare each other down...hard. It is an epic struggle. It is none other than the classic struggle for Primacy.

See, the Alpha Male job is up for grabs. Beau has seen the Old Male limping to the bathroom in the morning, and he senses his time is coming. It is still technically my job. I've still got the mantle, but I can sure enough see the writing on the wall. I can maybe limp along for another year or two on bravado and bluster, but the outcome is preordained. It the Primate Way. And we are nothing if not balls-to-the-wall Primates.

Fortunately, it's all stylized. In our family, in this age, it is just a ritualized drama. Otherwise we would fight. Eventually I would get hurt. Bad. And then I'd have to go out into the forest and wait for the scavengers to come get me. An ugly ending.

◆ ◆ ◆

His class read *Of Mice and Men* this semester. He was reading it on a soccer road trip to Memphis. As he got closer and closer to end of the book, I could feel him becoming increasingly nervous as Steinbeck directed his poor players to their inevitable conclusion. When he finally finished, he put the book down, turned away. He stared out the window and watched the flat Mississippi delta roll by for a long time.

"It's not fair," he finally said. And of course he's right. It's a World full of injustice and sadness, and it's important to know that. And it's also important to understand guys like Lenny and George. They had a right to a better fate. Damn straight. They had a right to 10 acres somewhere with a little house and a vegetable garden and some chickens. Lenny had a right to a life that wasn't so hard and some rabbits to pet. It is absolutely important to understand that and to feel that.

And I am satisfied that Beau does. He gets the interplay between Confidence and Humility, and how they are appropriate at different times. Strength and Empathy are skills to be utilized each in their own way, their own time. He has shown me that he possesses each of these and knows the Power of all of them. And that he will use them judiciously. Of this I have no doubt.

And having proclaimed this, The Throne, such as it is, is his for the asking.

The Great Beyond

...in which Uncle Duke looks into Dying.

It has come to my attention that I may, at some point, die. It is a preposterous notion, I realize, given my current state of vigor and vitality. But I am assured, on good authority, that it is quite inevitable.

Now I can't say I ever actually considered myself immortal; but at the same time, I've never actually contemplated the final act, the curtain going down, the fat lady singing, checking out. And I have not yet grasped its full significance. But I will allow that it is worthy of some consideration, on a number of levels. If for no other reason, I'd like my wake done right. The way I understand it, you only get to do it once. It's not like a wedding or something.

A wake is not something you want planned by guys who wear blue suits and drive black cars to work every day. Nor do you want to give an absolutely free hand to your significant other, the one who continually tries to give away your favorite sport coat before you die. It is a very individual thing, Death. We all live highly individualistic, highly personalized lives, rich in texture and nuance and theme. And then our deaths, our final send-off, our big going away party, comes out of a cookie cutter.

Well not this corpse. I have some strong opinions on how we treat our most silent majority, and I demand a voice in my own final party. I am, after all, the host.

First of all, no chemicals. I was born with blood in my veins and I'd just as soon go out that way. Here I've been recycling and composting all these years, and I want to become Class II Hazardous Waste when I'm buried??? I don't think so! Consequently, this will be a one-night gig. I don't intend for this to be a farewell tour. So all my out-of-town friends better book early.

I do intend to be buried, by the way. Fire has never been a comforting prospect for me. I don't identify with ashes. On the other hand, I have always had a strong affinity for dirt. There is something very appealing about returning to the earth. We are all mostly comprised of organic molecules which come directly from the Earth and are constantly passing through us. In the end, we don't own any of the stuff that we are made of. It is all borrowed material we've used to make cells with. Death is just the completion of the cycle. We just go back to where we came from. So the thought of my remains being broken down and taken up and becoming tree bark and deer antlers and sweet corn is appealing to me and entirely consistent with my views of a rich and satisfying after-life. In some ways I'm looking forward to it.

Which brings me to the subject of caskets. It is unconscionable to me that we bury our dead in elaborate and expensive vaults, airtight and watertight. And then we put the whole shebang in a concrete vault, lined with copper or stainless steel. In the event of a direct nuclear hit, our dead are well protected. But what's the point here? We destroy ecosystems to make mahogany and teak and bronze caskets to bury our dead in. You want a real good definition for vanity and arrogance? That one works for me.

I myself would prefer a pine box. It's cheap and plentiful. Scrap lumber would be better yet. Beau does wonderful stuff with old pallets. Even cardboard would be acceptable, I suppose. Lord knows there's enough of it around we can't figure out what to do with. But actually, the thought of being laid out in my living room with Frigidaire running the length of my final resting place is aesthetically unpleasing. No, a pine box would be fine. And it will serve a dual purpose as my friends will no doubt all be overcome with grief and guilt for not being nicer to me while I was alive and ask if they can do anything. This will give them something to do. They've got all those fancy tools they never use anyway. And it will give them something to think about as well. There are a lot of little decisions to make—what kind of joints to make, screws, nails or glue. How would old Duke like it lined... blah, blah, blah. Good craftsmanship and attention to detail would be appreciated, though I'm aware of the temporal constraints. Do the best you can.

And one more thing. The guys at the hardware store will try and talk you into Wolmanized. Thanks anyway. Untreated is fine. I'd like to get this decomposition thing going as soon as possible. It sounds liberating to me. I have no intention of being reincarnated, at least in this body. My knees are shot, my teeth are worn out and my athlete's foot fungi give every indication that they will outlive me, no matter how many times I come back.

Yes, by the way, I do intend on having the wake at my house. Death is the most personal of things, and it is best done in your own home. You spend all those years paying for it–why rent space? And I would be more relaxed there. Parking could be a problem. The street is not really set up for such huge crowds. But a nice, brisk walk would do my relatives good. And my friends could all use the exercise. Unless they pre-decease me. In which case, they shouldn't much care.

Transportation is another issue. The traditional hearse has never done much for me. I've never said: "Boy, I can't wait to ride in one of those!" It is a gas-guzzler, and it looks so damn somber. I bet they don't let you ride in it for free either. No really, if I want to ride in a limo, I'll rent one for my birthday. For my funeral, it seems to me a pick-up is made to order. Just slide me in the back of my truck there. I'll be fine. It's not like I'll get cold or anything.

Now how does one dress for one's own wake? Generally I prefer casual, but it does seem that for your final bash, your big *Bon Voyage*, you ought to bring out your best. Why hold back? It's your last chance to look good. I say, pull out all the stops. If you own a tux, wear it. I'm planning on renting. As I say, you only die once.

There are so many details and so little time. I really should have begun this a long time ago. They say it's never too late. But the point is, I guess, that at some point it is too late. Death creeps up and we largely deny it and defend against it and treat it like an alien. We fear our own demise almost as much as we fear getting old. It doesn't make sense of course, our fear of the inevitable, but we do it anyway. Out of force of habit. Which is the same way we treat our wakes. We back into them with our eyes squinched tight. The last thing on our lists, we never get around to the planning. We allow strangers to take over our final task.

Well friends, consider this my Last Will and Testament. I'm no smarter than anybody else, so I'll probably never get around to the real kind. You are all my Witnesses here. I am within some nominal and legal bounds of sanity. Let it be known that my eyes are wide open. My wishes are hereby and forthwith printed above in black and white. And they are that I close it out with an exclamation point. When I buy the farm, I want it done right, with style and a proper modicum of taste. You're all invited. Gentlemen please wear ties.

Weeds and Other Demons

...in which Uncle Duke advocates moderation.

I'd like to go on record right now as saying I don't see anything wrong with a little tobacco. Having said that however, I do not dispute that there are very real health problems associated with the product. Inhaling huge quantities of anything except relatively clean air is a definite threat to lungs and other associated organs. Living inside dense clouds of smoke, whether first or second hand, is inadvisable in both the short and long run of it. I do not dispute this.

I do dispute however those who would reach in and condemn the substance because some people abuse it. There are few moments in life to compare to a quiet, uninterrupted smoke. Moments of reverie, looking out through a rich cloud of tobacco smoke, set aside moments in which one is not expected to do anything other than savor the slight intoxication, the heady, deep pleasure of tobacco curling about. Inside these moments are pleasures which are religious in nature and inspirational for the soul. Inside these tranquil recesses is theology at its finest.

What is wrong with tobacco is not the tobacco itself, or even the nicotine. It is the profit motive that turned a sturdy, inoffensive weed which the Native Americans discovered could be lit and inhaled into a megapackaged and insidiously advertised accessory in a crush-proof box. Somebody sold us menthol taste, micronite filters, snappy slogans and romantic billboards, and we bought them by the carton-full. They took a local product that was grown in little patches behind the house and made it into a full-fledged industry with stockholders and boards of directors. In America's finest tradition, they told us that if we used it, we would be more confident and more popular. They said the more we used, the cooler we would be. Whatever our personalities lacked, whatever image we wanted to project, why there was a brand out there that would provide it. They sold us a bill of goods, and we bought it. By the cartonful.

The point here is that tobacco is yet another product abused by America's obsessive-compulsive personality. If it feels good, do it til it kills you. Butterscotch sundaes are wonderful things. But we don't chain-eat them all day long. Tobacco can be a pleasant additive to life. But not if it consumes 10% of our gross income and fills our lungs and the lungs of those around us with choking particulates. The industry just made it spectacularly easy to smoke, and we are absolute suckers for ease. The easier it is, the more we tend to abuse it. And the more we abuse it, the less we appreciate it. We stopped savoring tobacco generations ago.

In earlier times, we used to roll our own. It required time and concentration, both of which lent themselves to enhancing the tobacco experience. And there was a certain skill involved, certainly a point of pride. But unless one is absolutely stationary, there is an upper limit to how many roll-yer-owns one can do in a day. It was few enough that the roller would be mostly removed from cancer statistics. And the addictive effects were minimized. I had an aunt who rolled one cigarette a day for most of her adult life. I never saw anyone enjoy a smoke as much as her in my life. And my assumption is that she would have had to have lived a lot longer than 94 for it to have killed her. I rest my case.

There are other pleasures in life that have been similarly sullied. Drugs come to mind. Various drugs have properties that can lead to self-revelation, that can, properly used, provide valuable perspective. In combination with an inquiring mind and a spiritual base, drugs can enhance enlightenment. Early religions used certain drugs in this manner.

With the increase in the level of pain in our society, drugs have become heavy-duty anesthetics. Persistently bombing the brain with atomic mega-blasts is obviously not of great benefit to the individual or the culture. It provides momentary relief but lingering, significant side effects. Charred lives lay along the roadside, and you got to blame something. Drugs become BAD. Well I don't particularly relish defending substances that can destroy lives, but it is not the drug that is the real villain here. The Mind is the thing. The Pain is the thing. The Emptiness is the thing. Drugs ain't the thing.

The same can be said for alcohol. There are numerous studies that have extolled the benefits of moderate alcohol intake. Indeed the pleasures of beer with barbeque or wine with dinner or sipping whiskey at bedtime are considerable. I have however tripped over enough muscatel bottles, been panhandled enough and read enough sad statistics to know that it doesn't end there. The human condition being what it is, there is a tendency to use it to seek psychological release. And nothing delivers momentary liberation like copious quantities of alcohol. It is cheap enough and darned effective.

The advertising people imply that drinking is somehow associated with attractive young women with large breasts. They are, in fact, not related. Neither is it related to cold, mountain streams or wild mustangs. Mostly it is related to inducing as many of us as possible, by cheap hook or clever crook, to drink as much of the product as possible. What was once made out of dandelions and potatoes down in the cellar and used for barter and special occasions is now sold by the case in gas stations and has become the national sedative.

Well it's comforting to have a scapegoat, and alcohol is pretty handy. But it's the sadness and the fear and the uncertainty that make us turn to it in such quantity. A Constitutional Amendment prohibited the alcohol, but it didn't touch the despair.

So in this national debate over *"What's wrong with America?"*, I think it is important to remember that it is not the abuse of drugs that precipitated moral decay—more likely the other way around. It is not profligate sex and out-of-control rock 'n' roll which caused declining family values, but the opposite. It is not the misuse of alcohol which brings about spiritual emptiness, but vice versa. The focus must be clear before the cure can be effected.

Natural Gas

…in which Uncle Duke recounts a near-death experience.

If you recall, I have written previously about farting. I find it the funniest thing in the known Universe. No Exceptions. And I am completely unapologetic about this. I believe farts are our Original Joke. The one thing that all of us are hardwired to laugh at. They are punch lines that need no joke. Education, titles, religion, political affiliation–none of that matters. Age? Kindergartners giggle. Geezers wheeze and cackle. We are all, young and old, servants to the Universal, Cosmic fart. Throughout our History too, I'm convinced. Cro-Magnon girls, Neanderthal guys, sitting in a cave. When one of them ripped a shaggy one, and it echoed off the walls...they'd all be on their backs holding their hairy bellies. Queen Elizabeth laughs when royalty biffs. I saw it on YouTube. So does the Pope. For sure. All those old Cardinals around him all the time, you know the air is thick with fish-on-Friday farts. Whoo-whee! And nothing's funnier than nun flatulence. Yuk-yuk! The more inappropriate the better. Who-o-ops! Even the silent and deadly ones. Or perhaps especially the s & d's. To see that growing awareness come over people's faces when they realize they are being engulfed in a toxic cloud. Trapped inside a real-life whoopee cushion. That evolving look of horror, that wide-eyed, looking-for-an-exit, panicked response is as funny as it gets. It is virtually the only time I laugh out loud anymore.

I bring this up because of a particularly horrific/hilarious event in spinning class the other morning. I was huffing and puffing along when all of a sudden I realized I was in the middle of a singularly vile and gag-awful fart zone. Someone in the class (and there were only five of us) had quietly let one of the most revolting little bombs I can ever recall. And I remember most of them. It was awful. It was reprehensible. It was subhuman. This was a screamin' meemie, I tell you. A real rip-snorter. A blue darter. A hum dinger of the first order. This fart was Bad to the Bone and looking for victims. And bear in mind that I was breathing hard, hard, hard. I was in Stage 4 oxygen deprivation. Holding my breath was not an option. So I was gulping in great quantities of this swamp gas completely against my will. This paint peeler was now in my lungs and creating who-knows what kind of permanent, internal damage. My trachea was blistering. My whole cardiovascular system was at risk. My eyes burned and teared up as I looked wildly around for relief. I looked toward the door, but I knew I'd never make it. I had to ride it out. Except...it didn't go away. If anything, it was getting stronger. It was gaining in potency. It was like a massive, malodorous high pressure system had just settled in over St. Louis. Hell, over the whole Mississippi Valley for all I knew. It was a mushroom cloud of a fart. A volcanic plume. Understand that there were four high-output, overhead fans going at the time. They're like helicopter rotors. And they were totally useless. This, my friends, was a 500 pound gorilla, a monster fart that was not about to budge. This was the Bubonic Plague of farts. This epic mega-bomb, this Sasquatch of cheese balls, this foul wooly mammoth of a fart, this Godzilla fart had barged in, made a nest and, I swear to God, started having babies. AAAARRGGGHHH!!!

I looked around the room. There was a short list of suspects. I'm pretty sure it was the middle aged lady next to me. The one with the helmet hair and the shorts with the little rabbits on them. She looks like she has an odd diet. Like she might eat a lot of cabbage and corn dogs. Or maybe road kill. Possum maybe. Whatever. Whew!

Anyway, as much as I was panicking, I was also involuntarily laughing so hard that I began to snort and make weird wheezing noises. So I'm sucking air, trying to get oxygen to my bloodstream, but this fart had sucked all the oxygen out of the room so now I'm blowing out my good air in uncontrolled laughter cause I know it's her and I'm starting to see the rabbits jump ship, the bunnies are freaking baling, but maybe I'm just delirious from asphyxiation. Meanwhile, she ignores all this and pedals on, looking straight ahead. She is actually getting stronger. She is obviously immune to her own farts. She is thriving, like some form of primitive bacteria that live on methane. Then I realize she's making a run for it. She's speeding up. She's trying to leave the scene on her stationary bike. The CO_2 detectors begin to blare and flash, so I pull her over. "No good, sister." I imagine saying, in my silent-but-deadly cop voice. "We know you dealt it. You can run but you can't hide!"

Well, it finally went away. Kind of. The fans do their job and finally shuffle those god-awful, cesspool molecules in with the standard ones. So it was tolerable, at least. But it had pretty much soaked into the carpet by then, so I bet the 7:30 class was still looking around for a dead and decaying polecat in the closet when they came in.

What a morning! Nothing like good, cheap, low-brow entertainment and the capacity to appreciate it, I tell you.

A Kind of Redemption

…in which Uncle Duke is at long last redeemed.

I have not led an entirely exemplary life. It's a popular perception, I know. And it is true enough that I've been a decent sort. I don't abuse small animals or heave trash out the car window. I try to do something nice for my wife on Valentine's Day and seldom smoke cigars in elevators. I tip pretty well and never (hardly ever) park in handicapped spaces. I mostly try to do the right thing. As I see it. But in the end, I am like the majority of the population, animals of my breed. I am ruled by my own insecurities and I've often acted accordingly. I am convinced that insecurities run the world. They shout out loudly our own needs and drown out the small voices of the weak and the timid, the gentle and the unremarkable…voices like Joe McWhorter's.

Joe was a year younger than me, and he was always slightly odd. His eyes didn't focus quite right. They were a little askew. They weren't what you'd call crossed, but they weren't straight-at-you eyes either. And he wore these glasses that were thick and heavy and always held together with electrical tape.

Joe's clothes never fit right. They were baggy and overly long at a time when baggy and overly long was not the style. They had the look of clothes that had come down from one of his cousins who was already in high school. His feet seemed too big for his body and kind of splayed out to the sides. He kind of waddled when he walked, and he ran like a duck. Joe was decidedly un-athletic at a time when status was overwhelmingly dependent on athleticism. He'd play keep-away with us, but it was not a fair game. The playing field was most decidedly tilted, and Joe McWhorter was always running uphill. It was painfully easy to keep it away from him. We'd run circles around him and hold the ball out to him. We'd make him look sillier than he usually did. His glasses would fall off and his pants legs would flap. "*Quack, quack,*" we'd taunt. He'd pull up his pants and play on though. I will say he never gave up, chasing us around til the recess bell would ring.

There was something about Joe that invited abuse. He was such an easy target. We honed our sarcastic skills at Joe's expense. If there was a lull in the conversation, someone could always think of something stupid Joe had done. Or was doing. He took it so well. Not that he had much choice.

Neither was Joe very bright. That year, I was in a combined class with him. Fourth and fifth grades. I would watch him struggle for right answers in front of the class. He would sweat and shuffle and squint and swallow. He really wanted a correct answer, something to get him off the hook. And he might have even known the answer. I think he really did study. But for whatever reason, the right answers wouldn't come to him when he was in front of the class. He was a fish out of water up there. He'd have sold his soul on the spot for a little approval. I don't ever recall it happening though. Mostly what he got was humiliation and snickers from all of us other mental giants.

In my own defense, I will say I was never a ringleader. I don't remember being the instigator, the main agitator. But I merrily joined in. I was always more than happy to heap more abuse on poor, old Joe. I sold him down the river more than once for a little peer approval.

◆ ◆ ◆

Well the long and short of this sad story is that Joe died in Vietnam. He made it out of high school somehow and immediately enlisted in the Marines. I have no idea how he got in, with his feet and his eyes. But he did. He was no doubt aching to get out of that small town. It is my assumption that this was his chance to redeem himself, to forge his un-athletic body into a hard, sharp-edged fighting machine, to fill out his chest, get into a proud, tight-fitting uniform and assume a new identity. This was his attempt to stand tall and become an object of praise and admiration.

It may have happened, too. I don't know. But if it did, it was brief and confined to a small paddy in the Far East. People who make speeches for a living talk about this kind of heroism all the time. "The price of liberty is dear," they say. Well I'm not sure it was liberty we were buying, but Joe McWhorter paid the price. And the sorry, bitter truth is that Joe McWhorter was expendable. His death was one of thousands that came to unremarkable boys all across America back then. There were brief expressions of sympathy and sorrow, but the war and life ground on. And pretty soon he was just another cross on a hill.

◆ ◆ ◆

And that pretty much would have been the end of the story. I hadn't thought about Joe for years, until I saw his father at the nursing home. I was visiting my aunt when I noticed him wandering up the hall. R.C. McWhorter had been a mechanic. He was a tall, laconic man with huge ears who listened intently, with a kind of a half grin on his face, while you told him what was wrong with your car. Then you'd go away, and when you got back it would be fixed. He was honest and good at what he did. When I saw him again, he was still tall and still had those big-knuckled mechanic's hands. Even now there looked like there was a little grease under his nails that just wouldn't come out. But his shoulders stooped and there was no life left in his eyes.

Someone noticed him moving in my direction and brought him to my attention. "You remember R.C., don't you," they said, like he wasn't really there. "His son Joe got killed in 'Nam and he's never really gotten over it." He heard that. There was nothing wrong with those ears. He stopped moving and looked up at me. "And I never will either," he said. Then he shuffled on back down the hall.

I had missed all that–all those middle years of McWhorter history, from grade school on through the nursing home. I had been out making a life–going to college, getting deferred, missing Vietnam. I moved away and the McWhorters were just shadows of a former life. Joe had died and R.C. had become one of those guys who ate when someone told him it was time, who went to the bathroom if he really had to, and then went to bed when they turned out the lights. He was just a guy waiting for the lights to permanently go out.

At some point in my own personal history, I became a father. And right then my life deepened. So when I saw R.C.'s large, sad, empty eyes, I was transfixed. All at once I understood it all, as if, when he looked at me, he'd told me the whole story. Every detail. I saw it all through his eyes. I could see him standing up on the hill, overlooking our playground, watching us boys at recess. I could hear the taunts and the snickers. I could see us dancing around Joe, waving the ball in his face and mocking him. I saw him waddle after us. Quack, quack echoed in my head. It cut right to my soul. And I was suddenly ashamed. Ashamed that I hadn't been the one to be Joe McWhorter's friend. Ashamed that I had taken the easy way. Ashamed that I hadn't put my arm around him and picked him on my team.

Stepping up, they call it now. I was ashamed I hadn't stepped up. Not even once.

I remember seeing R.C. pick his son up once after school. Joe ran up to him and unashamedly wrapped his spindly arms around R.C.'s waist. R.C. tussled his hair. They got in the truck, and R.C. took Joe's glasses off and pulled out a roll of tape. Even then, I recall being momentarily touched at the scene of a son in the safe, accepting presence of his father, a man who loved him above all else. But in the end, in my 5th grade world, it was just another sign of Joe's weakness. It was just another soft spot to use against him.

I guess I don't apologize for being human. And I don't suppose I'm necessarily ashamed of my imperfect human traits or acting in the way the World prompted me to act. The Powerful have always tormented the Weak. We ally ourselves with the strong, however stupid, in order to avoid mockery or worse. Our insecurities, our fears of being on the outside looking in, push us to act like cowards more often than not. We are social animals, intimidated by the majority. It is the Way of the World. But I would like to have been smarter than that. I would like to have been wiser. I would like to have had the courage to have changed a very small portion of the world in a very small way. Just once.

◆◆◆

Well, I carried the memory of Joe McWhorter and his dad around with me for most of my adult life. Carried the regret too. Then one day a number of years ago, I was talking to my son's teacher. Beau was in 5th grade. She happened to mention that she had noticed him on the playground. "He's a wonderful athlete and a real leader out there," she said. "But what really impresses me is that when he picks teams, he always chooses at least one other boy who isn't really very good. I tell you, it just makes their day."

I'm not sure what I felt really. I know I got kind of weepy-eyed, which I'm sure baffled Mrs. Wolf. The longer answer is that I've always felt that I was paying for mistakes of long-ago. Some ill-advised decisions, some less than courageous actions, have made my life more difficult at times. And I have compounded the problems. But now it would appear that present generations are repairing some of my own mistakes. There is a kind of justice in that, I think. There is a certain universal symmetry there that appeals to me and gives me hope.

I don't really believe in reincarnation. But I do believe in rejuvenation. Lessons learned are lessons served. We make mistakes, we move on. But if we live examined lives, we make corrections in ways which our children and others can see and understand and internalize. They become smarter, wiser, braver than we were. They make better choices. It is the Way of the World. In Time, there is Redemption. Excelsior!

WHO IS THIS MAN WHO LOVES YOU SO

On the stairs, at the foot of the stage
She waits for her name to be called.
.......“Margaret Mary Hardesty”.......
.......“Roger Nichols Hart”.......
Hearing it now...”Adele Louise Hathaway”...
she bounds up and onto the hardwood floor
toward the lectern.
She is short and thick
and there is little grace in her stride.
But there is energy aplenty
and immense purpose, so it seems.
For these are determined steps she now takes.
Arriving at center stage, she grasps Dr. Laslow's hand
and shakes it vigorously.
Her diploma in hand, she clunks across the remaining stage
and down the short stairs.

As she beams for the official photograph,
an elderly gentleman hurries down the auditorium stairs.
Before she charges out of the gate, he intercepts her.
And in a display so spontaneous
So unselfconscious and charming
so full of what we all need
he wraps her and her gown
and her diploma and her smile
and her energy
all up
all up
in an immense and protracted embrace.
It is genuine, delightful
and mutual.
Graduates pass them by.
Weeks and years pass.
Other lives and Time itself moves by.
Until she too draws away

from their world
– because she must–
to rejoin her world.

He is not well, it seems.
From the looks of him
he has not been well for some time.
He is still tall
but gaunt now
and pale.
And his suit belongs to a younger man
though it has held its crease
and waited patiently for just this day.
He has planned and arranged for this event.
To be here
he has summoned and harnessed energy.
But it is waning now
and he moves slowly
back up the stairs.

And I ask her: "Who is this man who loves you so?"
I ask this young woman, from my place across a great divide:
"Who is he? And how is his love so strong?
How did it come to be,
to reach across generations
and find you here?
When did he first know it?
Was it so full then? Or has it grown?
Is it done yet? Or has it only begun?"

"And you?
How does it feel to be so bathed?
How does it feel to be the source of such pride?
How does it feel to emit such light
that others can warm themselves by it?
Were you born into it?
Or have you earned it? Do you deserve it?

Is it as freely given, as unconditional, as it appears?
Is it always rich? Or is it a burden sometimes...this love?"

"You do understand he walks with you.
That he clears your path while you sleep.
He checks your oil each day
and minds your checkbook every Sunday.
It is he who butters your toast when you have no time."

And I say to her...
because I know such things...
I say to her: "Adele, you do deserve it.
It is innately earned.
This love is unadorned and unattached,
exactly as it seems.
It is inherited, gifted and unbeholden.
Wide and deep
it had no beginning
and there is no end to it.
It is yours for free and for all time,
for the asking
or without.

So rejoin your world, child.
But wear his love like a scarf.
Have it printed on all your cards.
Frame it and hang it on the wall
For all to see
Let it be your eternal banner
Never dulled, never diminished.
It is not done, dear.
It is only begun.

Author's Note

Duke Haydon was born and raised in Springfield, Kentucky, a town and a state to which he still pays allegiance. He has an English degree from St. Louis University and a Civil Engineering degree from SIU-Edwardsville and has been employed by the Innsbrook Corp. as the Project Engineer since 1980.

Duke lives in an old Victorian house in Lafayette Square in St. Louis City with his wife of 30+ years, Diana. She is a splendid lady, a valued friend and the mother of their sons, Caleb Jolly born in 1987–and Beau Baylor–1992. They are both fine young men. You would think so, too.

The pieces in the book have been written over a period of time. There was some effort made to keep them in chronological order, but not too much. They cover a range of topics, some factual, some inane. There is some Truth and some Heresy, for sure. But if Uncle Duke could generalize, the subjects he keeps returning to are Parenting, Love, Longing and Farting. The Big 4. It turns out that most of what Uncle Duke knows and values can somehow be found in one of those themes.

Made in the USA
Charleston, SC
29 February 2016